A World Beneath the Waves

Whales, Dolphins, and Porpoises

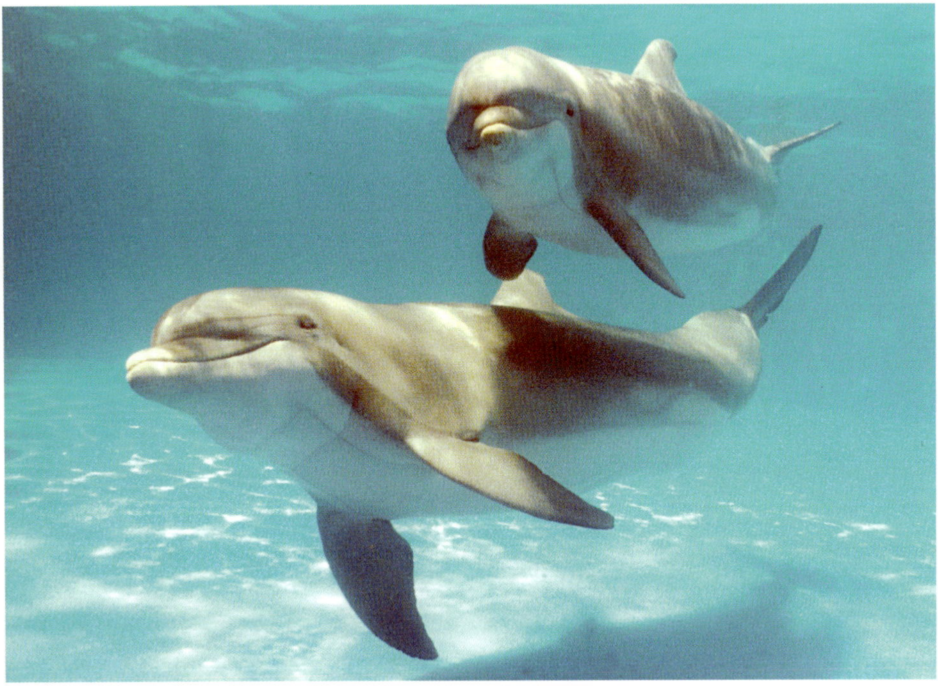

A World Beneath the Waves
Whales, Dolphins, and Porpoises
PART OF THE SEAWORLD EDUCATION SERIES

Research/Writing/Layout
Jody Byrum
Patricia Schick

Technical Advisors
Brad Andrews
Richard Baker
Ann Bowles
Dave Force
Tom Goff
Bill Hughes
John Kerivan
Jim McBain
Pat Sassic
Mike Scarpuzzi
Glen Young

Education Directors
Judy Jenkins
Ann Quinn
William Street
Sheila Voss
Joy L. Wolf

Editorial Staff
Tiffany Golota
Catherine Gregos
Deborah Nuzzolo
Loran Wlodarski

Illustrations
Doug Fulton
Noelle Phillips
August Stein
Chris Vine

Photos
Mike Aguilera
Andries Blouw, Fisheries and Oceans Canada
Bob Couey
Tui De Roy, Minden Pictures
Hubbs-SeaWorld Research Institute
Stephen Leatherwood
Flip Nicklin, Minden Pictures
Paul Ponganis
Patricia Schick
SeaWorld San Diego Photo Department

Photographs
Cover: A beluga whale.
Title page: Bottlenose dolphins are among the most familiar toothed whales.
Contents page, 106–107, 108–109, 112–113, 114–115: A blue whale flukes before it dives.
Page 1: A human diver is dwarfed by a gray whale calf.
Pages 12–13: Bottlenose dolphins live in fluid social groups.
Pages 28–29: Bottlenose dolphins can hear tones in the range of 1 to 150 kHz.
Pages 36–37: A killer whale leaps out of the water in a behavior called a bow.
Pages 52–53: A beluga whale.
Pages 76–77: Killer whale mother calf pair.

Acknowledgement
We gratefully acknowledge Randall R. Reeves, who granted us permission to use the photographs of the late Stephen Leatherwood.

©2006 SeaWorld, Inc. All Rights Reserved.
Published by the SeaWorld Education Department
500 Sea World Drive, San Diego, California, 92109-7904
ISBN 1-893698-01-7
Printed in the United States of America.

Contents

A World of Whales.................................1
Whales Inside and Out......................13
Whale Behavior 37
Species Spotlights............................53
Life and Death in the Sea..................77
Appendix: Whale Classification........106
Glossary..109
More Information............................112
Index..114

A World of Whales

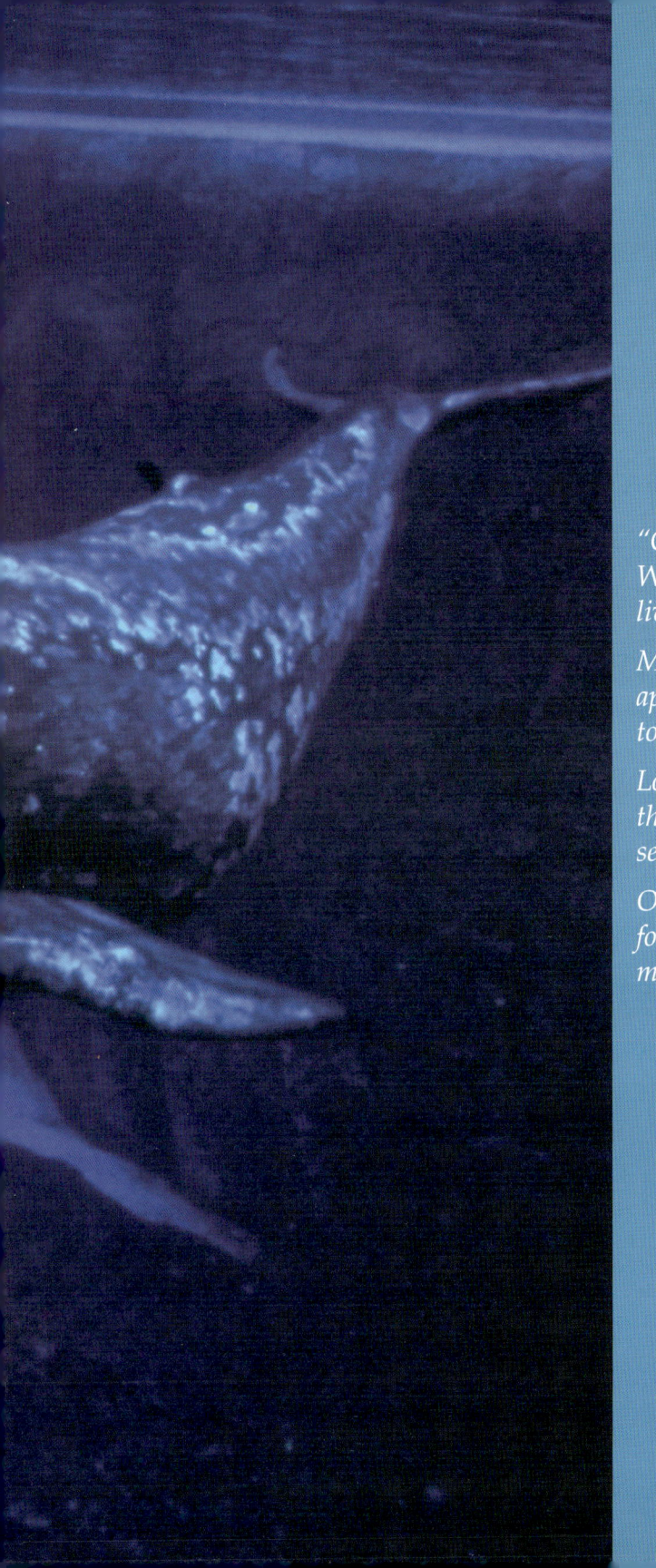

"Greatest of all is the Whale, of the Beasts that live in the waters,

Monster indeed he appears, swimming on top of the waves,

Looking at him one thinks, that there in the sea is a mountain,

Or that an island has formed, here in the midst of the sea."

Abbot Theobaldus

Bottlenose dolphins are one of the most familiar whales.

What is a Whale?

Probably no other creature has captured our fascination as much as the whale. Whales have been the subject of many folk legends and myths since long before the beginning of recorded literature. Whale imagery abounds in ancient artwork of virtually every coastal culture.

Even today, many people regard whales as ethereal, mystical creatures. This may be because no other animal possesses quite the same combination of beauty, power, grace, and curiosity. But to attribute supernatural characteristics to any animal is itself a mythical remnant. What are the facts about whales, and what is fiction? One of the most common misconceptions about whales is that, because they live in the water, they are fish. But whales are air-breathing, warm-blooded mammals. They must come to the surface to breathe, and they maintain a constant body temperature. They also bear live young, nurse their young, and even have hair at some point in their lives.

The 85 or more known species of whales, dolphins, and porpoises belong to the mammalian order Cetacea. Cetaceans share the characteristics of forelimbs modified into flippers, a horizontally flattened tail, one or two nostrils at the top of the head for breathing, and no hind limbs.

The earliest fossil whales have been estimated to be from about 50 million years ago. Scientists theorize that the ancestors of whales were ancient (now extinct) land mammals. Modern forms of toothed and *baleen* whales appear in the fossil record five to seven million years ago. Molecular and paleotological evidence suggest that the closest living relative to whales is the hippopotamus.

Is it a dolphin or a porpoise?

Dolphins are often mistakenly referred to as porpoises. Porpoises belong to a separate cetacean family, Phocoenidae. Porpoises differ from dolphins in several physical and behavioral characteristics. Dolphins tend to have tapered, beaklike snouts, or rostrums; porpoises have more blunt rostrums. Dolphins have sharp, conical teeth, while porpoises have spade-shaped teeth. And dolphins generally have curved-back, or falcate dorsal fins, while the dorsal fins of porpoises tend to be triangular. In some regions the terms "dolphin" and "porpoise" are used interchangeably in reference to any small toothed whale.

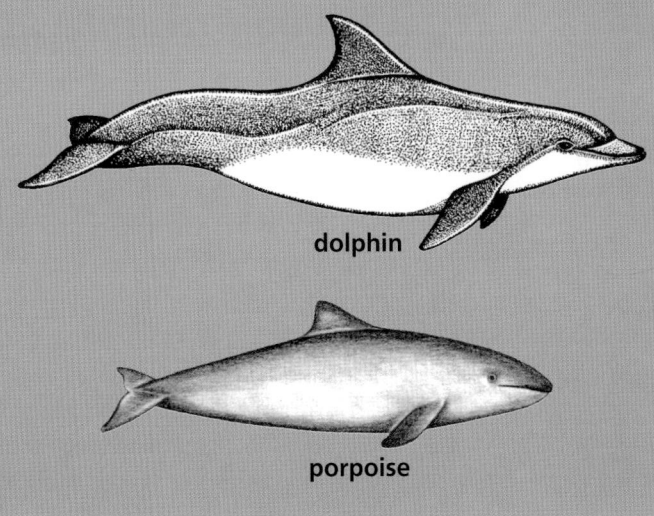

dolphin

porpoise

The baleen whales are among the largest mammals on earth. Pictured is a fin w

 Whale Family Album

Cetaceans are divided into two suborders—Odontoceti and Mysticeti—based on physical and behavioral differences between the whales.

The baleen whales.

Mysticeti is comprised of the four families of baleen whales (see page 6). Instead of teeth, baleen whales have long, stiff, bristly plates of *baleen*. These plates hang down along each side of a mysticete's upper jaw, resembling a mustache when the whale's mouth is open. The word "mysticete" may be derived from the Greek word for moustache, *mystakos*. Mysticetes are typically larger

than odontocetes ranging in size from the 6.1 m (20 ft.) pygmy right whale to the 27 m (90 ft.) blue whale. In general, female baleen whales grow larger than males. Unlike odontocetes, mysticetes have two *blowholes*. They also tend to be more solitary than toothed whales, only forming loose aggregations when feeding and migrating. The only lasting social bond is between a baleen whale mother and her calf.

The toothed whales.

The ten families of toothed whales form the suborder Odontoceti (see page 7). The word "Odontoceti" comes from the Greek word for tooth, *odontos*. Teeth may be conical, as in dolphins, or spade-shaped, as in porpoises. Odontocetes are relatively small compared to the mysticetes. Odontocetes range in size from about 1.5 m (4.9 ft.) for the vaquita, the Hector's dolphin, and the Commerson's dolphin to the 16 m (52.5 ft.) sperm whale. Among toothed whales, males typically grow larger than females. Unlike mysticetes, toothed whales have a single blowhole and tend to be social in nature, usually exhibiting complex social structures.

Many toothed whales, like the white-sided dolphin, are relatively small when compared with baleen whales.

Whale Families

There are 14 whale families in all—four baleen whale families and ten toothed whale families. They are classified based on several physical and behavioral differences. (For a complete list of species, see **Appendix**.)

Suborder Mysticeti (Baleen Whales)

Family Balaenidae
the right whales

Family Neobalaenidae
the pygmy right whale

Family Balaenopteridae
the rorqual whales

Family Eschrichtiidae
the gray whale

Suborder Odontoceti (Toothed Whales)

Sperm whales:
Family Physeteridae
the sperm whale (pictured)
Family Kogiidae
the pygmy and dwarf
sperm whales

Family Phocoenidae
the porpoises

Family Monodontidae
the beluga (pictured) & narwhal

Family Ziphiidae
the beaked whales

Family Delphinidae
the oceanic dolphins

River Dolphins:
Family Platanistidae
the Ganges & Indus
river dolphins
Family Iniidae
the Amazon river dolphin
Family Pontoporiidae
the franciscana
Family Lipotidae
the baiji (pictured)

Whales not drawn to scale.

Where Whales Live

Whales are found in every ocean of the world. Some whales even live in smaller bodies of water, including bays, lagoons, and certain river systems.

Baleen whales are found in all oceans, from polar seas to temperate and tropical zones. Most species of baleen whale have a worldwide distribution, although some species have a limited distribution. Bowhead whales inhabit the waters around the Arctic ice edges that melt and reform seasonally. Bryde's whales are generally found in tropical and subtropical zones. Southern right whales are found only in the southern hemisphere while northern right whales are found only in the northern latitudes.

Most toothed whale species inhabit temperate seas. However, several species can be found from polar seas to tropical zones. Some species have worldwide or nearly worldwide distributions. Sperm whales inhabit all deep oceans, from the equator to the poles. Bottlenose dolphins and false killer whales inhabit temperate and tropical waters throughout the world. Killer whales, while concentrated around the earth's poles, can often be found in small numbers throughout temperate and tropical zones.

In contrast, some toothed whale species have very limited distributions. The vaquita lives only in the northernmost portion of the upper Gulf of California. The tucuxi inhabits the waters of northeastern South America from Brazil to Panama, and ranges into large river systems. Irrawaddy dolphins live in coastal areas of the Indo-Pacific and southeast Asia, where they range into large rivers including the Irrawaddy, Mekong, and Ganges. Some toothed whales are found entirely in freshwater river systems. The boto inhabits the Amazon and Orinoco river systems of South America. Ganges River dolphins range in the Ganges, Brahmaputra, and Karnaphuli River systems, while Indus River dolphins inhabit the middle and lower Indus River. The baiji's already limited range has recently shrunk to only the middle section of China's Yangtze River.

Habitat.

All marine habitats—and some freshwater habitats—are home to one or more cetacean species. Oceanic species of both baleen and toothed whales roam the open sea while coastal species prefer shallow, inshore waters. Some coastal species include the gray whale and Commerson's dolphin. Coastal cetacean species are accustomed to varying levels of salinity as marine waters mix with fresh. Adapted for shallow-water, nearshore habitats, coastal toothed whales may frequent harbors, bays, estuaries, and lagoons. River dolphins roam certain freshwater or brackish areas, including lakes, rivers, and mangrove swamps.

Killer whales inhabit oceans throughout the world, but are more commonly seen near the polar latitudes.

Whales on the Move

Most baleen whales are highly migratory, traveling to high latitude (polar) feeding areas in the summer and to lower latitude (tropical) calving areas in the winter. Many factors act as environmental cues to help whales navigate along a migration route: sun orientation, ocean floor topography, temperature and chemical changes in the water, food availability, and magnetic sensing. Satellite-tracking studies help scientists document the migratory behavior of baleen whales.

Migrations for most baleen whales average 3,000 to 5,000 km (1,800–3,000 mi.) each way, depending on the species. In one of the

**Gray whales undergo the longest migration of any marine mammal.
Photo by Patricia Schick.**

Bryde's whales undertake much shorter migrations; moving from temperate to tropical waters. Photo by Patricia Schick.

longest migrations of any marine mammal, gray whales migrate more than 10,000 km (6,214 mi.) from Alaskan waters to Baja California, Mexico. Other whales migrate much shorter distances. Bryde's whales only move from sub-temperate waters to the equator. Some juveniles and post-reproductive individuals do not migrate at all and remain in foraging grounds.

Some species of toothed whales also migrate. Narwhals travel north in the spring to the edges of fast ice in the fjords of North Baffin Island and northwest Greenland. In the fall they move south to Davis Strait, where they stay throughout the winter. Sperm whales are the only toothed whales that have been documented to regularly travel long distances. Groups of young males move toward the equator in autumn and to temperate waters in spring. Small groups of large males continue all the way to polar waters in the summer. Some toothed whales, such as coastal populations of bottlenose dolphins, stay within a limited home range. Other toothed whales make seasonal movements in response to variations in water temperature and food availability.

Whales—Inside and Out

"The sea is cold, but the sea contains the hottest blood of all."

from "Whales Weep Not!"
by D.H. Lawrence

Basic Whale Features

Though all whales share many basic similarities, each species has a variety of unique traits.

As big as a whale.

Whales range extensively in size. The smallest whales are the vaquitas, Commerson's dolphins, and Hector's dolphins that reach lengths of about 1.5 m (4.9 ft.). In contrast, some baleen whales, such as the gigantic 27 m (89 ft.) blue whale, are the largest animals on Earth. The record size for a blue whale, a female taken during whaling years, was 34 m (110 ft.). Another record-sized individual weighed 172,330 kg (380,000 lb.)—larger than the estimated size of any dinosaur yet discovered. The heart of an average-sized blue whale probably weighs about 322 kg (710 lb.), and the heart of a larger individual may weigh more than 680 kg (1,500 lb.), the weight of a small car.

Because land animals must support their own weight, their size is limited by the force of gravity acting upon them. In an aquatic

Averaging more than 23 m (75 ft.), the blue whale is probably the largest animal that ever lived, but most people never see more than its head and back. Photo by Patricia Schick.

Commerson's dolphins are among the smallest cetaceans. They rarely exceed 1.5 m (5 ft.) and 45 kg (100 lb.).

environment, water helps support an animal's weight, allowing the potential for greater size. As an animal increases in size, its ability to retain body heat also increases. The larger body mass, producing metabolic heat, is surrounded by a relatively smaller surface area (the skin) to conduct that heat to the environment. So, large size is a metabolic advantage. Large size also allows an animal to eat a great deal of food and store excess energy for future use in the form of blubber.

In general, female baleen whales are 5% longer than males of the same species, and some species exhibit size differences depending on the stock. In the northern hemisphere, baleen whales tend to be slightly smaller than their southern hemisphere counterparts.

Toothed whales are generally smaller than baleen whales. The largest toothed whale is the sperm whale. *Bulls* (mature males) reach lengths of 16 m (52.5 ft.) and may weigh as much as 40,800 kg (90,000 lb.). In general, male odontocetes grow larger than females, although the reverse is true for some river dolphin, porpoise, and oceanic dolphin species and most beaked whale species. As with baleen whales, size variation often exists between different populations of a toothed whale species.

Streamlined swimmers.

All whales show some variation on a characteristic *fusiform* (tapering toward each end) body shape. This body shape reduces drag and is energy-efficient for swimming.

The two forelimbs of a whale are modified into *pectoral flippers* that whales use mainly to steer and, with the help of the tail flukes, to stop. Pectoral flippers have the major skeletal elements of the forelimbs of land mammals, but they are shortened and modified. The skeletal elements are rigidly supported by connective tissue. Rorquals and gray whales have four digits instead of five; the thumb bones are absent. The shape of pectoral flippers varies among whale species. They may be broad and paddle-shaped, as in killer whales and most baleen whales; long, narrow, and tapering, as in pilot and humpback whales; relatively small and blunt, as in Commerson's dolphins and sperm whales; or spatulate and scalloped, as in the Ganges and Indus River dolphins. In narwhals and beluga whales the pectoral flippers are relatively short, with upturned tips. Humpback whale pectoral flippers are up to one-third of the whale's body length. Beaked whales have slight depressions or pockets along the body wall. This adaptation allows a beaked whale to hold its pectoral flippers tightly against its body and enhance its streamlined shape.

Each lobe of a whale's tail is called a *fluke*. Flukes are flat pads of tough, dense, fibrous connective tissue, completely without bones or cartilage. Most whales have a median notch in their flukes. However, most beaked whales lack a median notch. The up and down movement of a whale's flukes propel the animal forward through the water and, in some cases, even partially or completely out of the water.

Most whales have a fin on top of the back called a *dorsal fin*. Like the keel of a boat, the dorsal fin may help stabilize a whale as it swims at high speeds, but a fin is not essential to a whale's balance.

A whale's streamlined shape makes it a more energy-efficient swimmer.

The dorsal fin may be relatively large, as in the 1.8m (6 ft.) tall dorsal fin of adult male killer whales, or relatively small as in the sperm whale, blue whale, and beaked whales. Some other whales like the gray whale, beluga, and finless porpoise completely lack a dorsal fin. Like the tail flukes, the dorsal fin is made of dense, fibrous connective tissue, with no bones. The shape of the fin may be falcate or triangular. Some individuals may have irregular-shaped dorsal fins, which sometimes lean to the left or right.

Head and neck features.

The heads of whales vary widely in size and shape. Whales belonging to the same family tend to have similarly-shaped heads. Right whales have huge heads—one-fourth to one-third of the entire body length in adults. The narrow elongated upper jaw bones arch upward to house extremely long baleen. Rorquals have

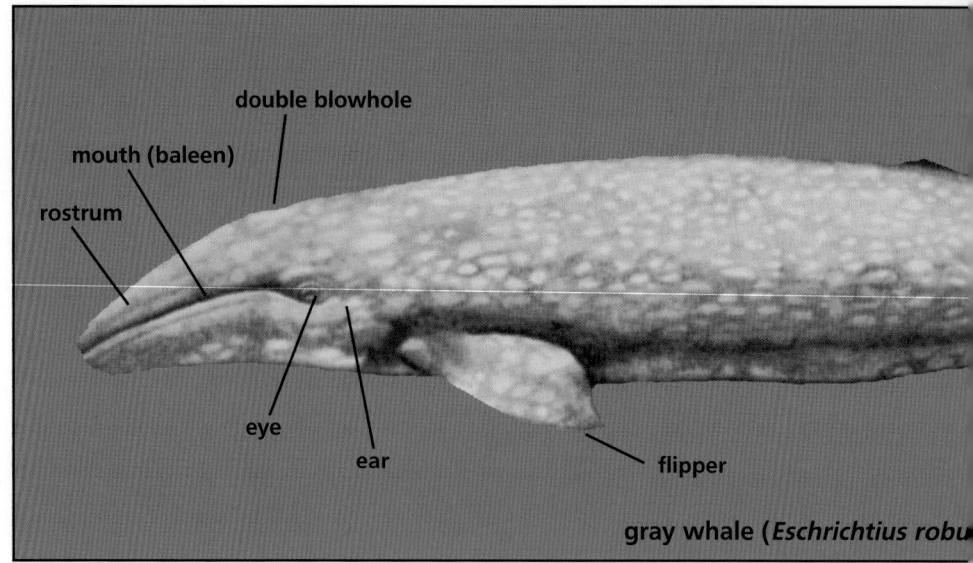

gray whale (*Eschrichtius robu*

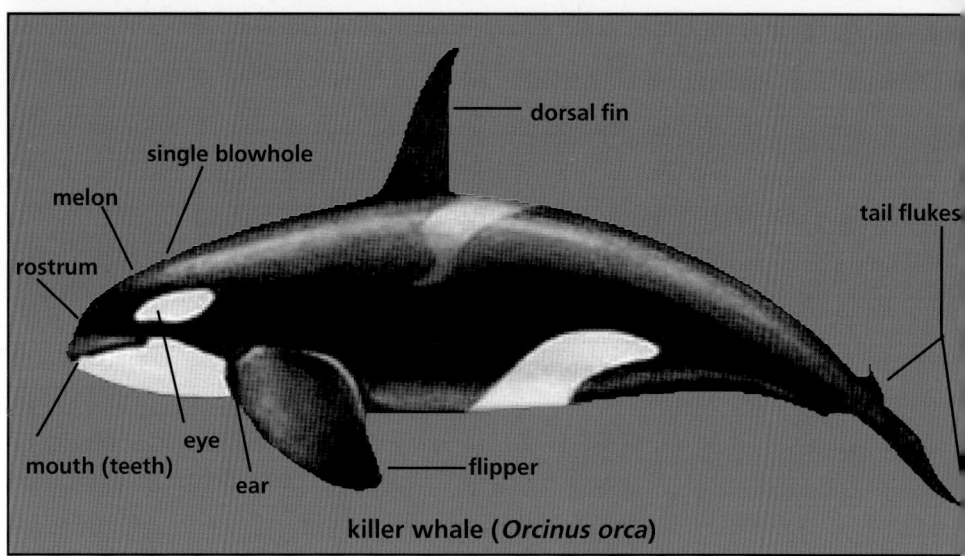

killer whale (*Orcinus orca*)

a broad, flat rostrum and a slightly curved jawline. Some species have ridges on the rostrum and a V- or U-shape to the tip of the snout. Humpback whales have several knobs on their heads while right whales have several raised and roughened patches of skin called *callosities* on their heads.

With the exception of the sperm whale, one feature that distinguishes a toothed whale is the rounded or bulging "forehead" area in front of the blowhole, called a *melon*. The melon is composed largely of fatty tissue, and is important in sound

tail flukes

production. Many toothed whales, including river dolphins, beaked whales, and most dolphins, also have a well-defined *rostrum*. Others, such as porpoises, sperm whales, beluga whales, narwhals, and some dolphins, have a blunt or rounded head.

The seven neck vertebrae of most whales are fused to various degrees, depending on the family. In the rorquals, gray whales, beluga, baiji, franciscana, and susus (Indus and Ganges river dolphins) all seven vertebrae are unfused, which allows greater mobility and flexibility of the neck. In most other whales, two to six of the neck vertebrae are fused, and they are incapable of side-to-side head movement. Only the first two vertebrae of the Irrawaddy dolphin are fused. In contrast, the last six vertebrae of the sperm whale are fused, giving a sperm whale a much more rigid body form.

A nose on top of the head.

All whales breathe through blowholes (modified nasal openings) located on top of the head. In sperm whales, the blowhole is located toward the left side of the head. Toothed whales have one blowhole; baleen whales have two. Blowholes may be

A beluga's unfused neck vertebrae allows greater flexibility and range of motion.

All whales breathe through blowholes on top of their heads. Toothed whales have one blowhole (left); baleen whales have two (right).

crescent-shaped, as in the bottlenose dolphins, longitudinal and straight, as in the river dolphins; or even S-shaped, as in the sperm whales.

Blowholes are covered by muscular flaps that provide a water-tight seal. Each blowhole opens to an air passage that leads to the animal's trachea and then to the lungs. The blowholes are in a closed position when relaxed. To breathe, whales must open their blowholes by contracting the muscular flaps that cover them. Some whale species have a "splash guard" in front of the blowhole region, which prevents water from entering the blowholes when surfacing to breathe. The visible spout of water that often rises from a whale's blowhole is not coming from the lungs, which (like ours) do not tolerate water. Instead, water collects on top of the closed blowhole. When a whale exhales, the water is forced up with the respiratory gases and, especially in cool air, a mist may form as water vapor condenses when the respiratory gases expand in the open air.

Making more room for a meal.

The rorquals, pygmy right whales, gray whales, sperm whales, and beaked whales have longitudinal skin folds, called throat grooves that extend from the throat to the flipper area. These folds expand the capacity of the mouth during feeding. The number of throat grooves may number two in pygmy right whales and beaked whales, two to seven in gray whales, two to ten in sperm whales, and 25 to 100 in rorquals.

Whale eyes and ears.

The eyes of a whale are on the sides of the head, near the corners of the mouth. The susus and the boto have extremely small eyes. A whale's eyes are constantly bathed in water. Although whales lack tear ducts, glands at the outer cornea and eyelids secrete an oily substance that lubricates and cleans the whales' eyes. Cetacean ears, located just behind the eyes, are small inconspicuous openings, with no external ear flaps, or pinnae.

Baleen: the natural strainer.

In mysticete whales, stiff plates of baleen grow down from the gums of the upper jaw. These plates are arranged in rows that extend down each side of the mouth. Baleen, sometimes called "whalebone," is made mostly of *keratin*—a protein-based substance

Gray whales have two to seven throat grooves. **Photo by** Patricia Schick.

that also composes hair, fingernails, hooves, and claws. Baleen is strong, yet somewhat elastic. The baleen plates are roughly triangular and arranged like the teeth of a comb. The outer edge (facing out) of each plate is smooth while the inner edge is frayed. The frayed edges intertwine to form a mat that functions as a strainer during filter feeding. Baleen whales mostly feed on tiny drifting animals called plankton. Many also consume small schooling fishes like herring and anchovies.

Baleen plates arise in the fetus as thickenings of the upper jaw skin. At birth, a calf's baleen is soft and short, but it soon stiffens. Baleen grows continually throughout a whale's lifetime, and the ends continually wear away. Baleen ranges in color from black to yellow or white, depending on the species. Its size and texture also vary, with some consistency among the four baleen whale families. Right whales—notably the bowhead whale—have the longest baleen. In bowheads, between 230 and 360 plates on each side of the jaw reach lengths of 4.3 m (14 ft.). Right whale baleen is also finely fringed, resembling human hair in texture. Rorquals have the coarsest baleen fringes, and baleen arrangements range in size and quantity. In blue whales, 270 to 395 black, baleen plates on each side of the upper jaw reach 1 m (3.28 ft.). Minke whales have 230 to 360, 12 to 20 cm (5 to 8 in.) black and white plates on each side. Gray whales

Fringed baleen plates hang from the upper jaws of mysticete whales. Pictured is a gray whale calf.

have about 130 to 180 whitish baleen plates on each side of the upper jaw, and each plate is 5 to 40 cm (2–15.7 in.) long.

Teeth: from function to legend.

Teeth are one key distinguishing characteristic of odontocete whales. Although baleen whales do not have teeth, they do develop tooth buds during the embryonic stage, which disappear before birth. Most odontocete whales have teeth adapted for grasping and tearing, but not chewing food.

The number and shape of teeth varies considerably among species and may even vary among individuals of the same species. Dolphins (Family Delphinidae) have conical, interlocking teeth; porpoises have spade-shaped teeth; and belugas have peg-shaped teeth. River dolphins have numerous small, sharp teeth well adapted for catching small fish. Amazon river dolphins also possess molarlike teeth in the back of their mouth to help them crush hard-bodied prey. Toothed whale species that eat predominantly squid tend to have far fewer teeth than those that mainly eat fish. Most male beaked whales have only one pair of teeth visible in the lower jaw, while functional teeth are usually absent in female beaked whales. Sperm whales have conical teeth in the lower jaw only, which fit into corresponding grooves in the upper jaw.

Odontocetes have anywhere from zero to 200 teeth.

One of the most remarkable examples of tooth specialization is the spiral tusk of the narwhal—the likely basis for the horn of the mythical unicorn. In adult male narwhals, the left tooth of the upper jaw develops into a spiral tusk that may be as long as 3 m (9.8 ft.) and may weigh more than 10 kg (22 lb.) The right tooth remains embedded in the upper jaw. In some cases, a male may have double tusks or none at all. In females, both teeth usually remain embedded in the jaw, though in rare cases females develop one or two tusks. Research is ongoing to determine the function of the narwhal's tusk.

Right whales (top) develop whitish bumpy growths called callosities around their faces. The skin of gray whales (bottom) is encrusted with barnacles and whale lice. Bottom photo by Patricia Schick.

Whale skin.

Typically whales have smooth, tight skin with few or no hairs. The epidermis (the outer skin layer) is 10 to 20 times thicker than in most terrestrial mammals. Most whales lose their hair either *in utero* (before birth), or just after birth. A whale's lack of fur is an adaptation for more efficient swimming since fur or hair creates drag as an animal swims. Some whales retain a few sparse hairs into adulthood. Humpbacks display prominent hair follicles, some with hairs, around their mouths. Some species have variations in skin texture. A sperm whale's skin is wrinkled over all except the head region of its body. Right whales develop characteristic whitish bumpy growths—called callosities—around their faces. Researchers can identify individual whales by the growth patterns of these callosities.

All whales shed their skin—most at a continuous, rapid rate. Skin sloughs off constantly and may feel slimy to the touch. Some species, like killer whales, rub their bodies on the bottom of shallow, pebbly shorelines. Scientists believe whales do this to aid in shedding skin. Unlike other whales, beluga whales appear to undergo a seasonal molt of the outer skin layer. During winter, a beluga's top skin layer may turn yellow, especially on its back and flippers. Rubbing on gravelly river bottoms helps a beluga shed this skin.

In most toothed whale species, light-colored parallel "rake marks" are common. These marks are made by one animal *raking* or scratching another with its teeth. Rake marks are the result of social interactions and are characteristic of the Risso's dolphin and Hubbs' beaked whale, among other species.

A variety of parasites can infest a baleen whale's skin. Diatoms grow on the skin of some large whale species, including the blue whale. Blue whales are sometimes called sulfur-bottoms in reference to the visible yellowish film of diatoms covering the skin on the whale's underside. Gray and humpback whales have *barnacles* encrusting parts of their bodies, particularly on their heads. Gray whales also have *whale lice* intermingled with the barnacles on their skin.

Countershading (top) allows a whale's back to blend in with the dark ocean depths, and its underside to blend with the lighter ocean surface. Disruptive coloration (bottom) disguises a whale's overall body shape in the filtered sunlight of the ocean.

Colors and patterns of whales.

Colors and color patterns vary among the whale species, but most whales exhibit some variation on black, white, and shades of gray. Some whales are spotted or mottled. The blue whale appears bright blue just beneath the water's surface, but is actually mottled blue-to slate-gray.

Many whales are *countershaded*: their dorsal surfaces are darker than their ventral surfaces. This coloration provides camouflage, making it difficult for predators and prey to spot them in an aquatic environment. If you are above a countershaded animal looking down toward it, its darker back may blend in with the dark ocean depths. If you are beneath the animal and looking up toward it, its lighter underside blends with the bright ocean surface.

Some whales, such as killer whales and Commerson's dolphins, exhibit *disruptive coloration*—contrasting color patterns that break up the general body shape and disguise the fins and flippers. In the flickering, filtered sunlight of the ocean, other animals may not recognize a disruptively colored one as a potential predator or prey.

An adult spotted dolphin's skin is patterned with lighter spots.

Whale Senses

The senses that whales have for perceiving their watery world are, in many ways, as different from those of land mammals as the marine environment is from the land.

Hearing.

Most whales probably have a well developed, acute sense of hearing. This is highly valuable in the ocean, where low light levels, especially at depth, greatly reduce the reliability of vision. Sound travels about 4.5 times faster in the water than it does in air, making it especially effective under water.

All whales have a tiny, external ear opening on each side of the head. These openings don't seem to play a role in conducting sound. Instead, bone and soft tissue are probably important in conducting sound to the ears.

In baleen whales, each ear opening leads to a narrow auditory canal that is completely plugged by a waxy substance. The ear attaches to the skull via bony connections, yet most of the ear lies outside the skull. The anatomy of the baleen whale ear is somewhat typical of an ear adapted to hear low-frequency sounds, although little is known about sound reception in mysticetes.

In contrast, the ears are not attached to the skull in most toothed whales. Ligaments hold each ear in a foam-filled cavity outside the skull. This separation of the ears allows a toothed whale to pinpoint high frequency sound, which is important for echolocation.

Sight.

Most whales have excellent vision in both water and air, although baleen whales are near-sighted in air. The retina of a whale's eyes contains mostly "rod cells," which are sensitive to low intensity light. "Cone cells," which distinguish between different colors and are most sensitive to bright light, are much less abundant. Scientists have found that many cetaceans lack S-cone cells and theorize that whales aren't able to discriminate color in the blue wavelengths. Scientists are not sure of the functional value for the lack in S-cone cells.

Although a whale's color vision may be more limited than a terrestrial animal's, the cetacean eye is extremely well adapted to vision in low light conditions. Whale eyes have a *tapetum lucidum*—

the reflective layer behind the retina that reflects light back through the retina a second time. This makes the most of available light under low light conditions—a particularly useful adaptation under the dark or murky water conditions whales often encounter when diving.

Not all whales see well. Some members of the river dolphin family are blind or nearly blind. The tiny eyes of Indus and Ganges river dolphins are virtually nonfunctional. Without a lens, at best they may be able to distinguish light from darkness. A baiji's eyes are also reduced and almost nonfunctional, while a boto's small eyes are functional. Most of the river dolphins inhabit waters thick with silt and keen eyesight is of much less importance than to oceanic cetaceans. Instead, these dolphins tend to rely more on echolocation to navigate and find food.

Touch.

Many whales have a well developed sense of touch, although this sense has not been well studied in baleen whales. Gray whales in certain breeding lagoons in Baja California, Mexico seem to seek out people and solicit interaction including touch. So far we lack an accurate interpretation for this behavior.

Studies and observations show that at least some toothed whales are sensitive to a broad range of tactile sensations. Studies of common dolphins, bottlenose dolphins, and false killer whales suggest that the most sensitive areas of these toothed whales are the blowhole region and areas around the eyes and mouth. Some scientists speculate that the sparse hairs on some toothed whales' rostrums may be sensory.

Taste and smell.

Little is known about a whale's sense of taste or smell. Cetaceans do have taste buds at the base of the tongue, although taste sensitivity has not been well studied. In zoological parks, whales and dolphins show strong preferences for specific food fishes.

Olfactory nerves and bulbs are present only in baleen whale fetuses— they are greatly reduced in adult baleen whales and absent in toothed whales. When present, researchers have not determined if such nerves and bulbs are functional, but toothed whales probably lack a sense of smell.

Survival in a Watery World

Survival is a challenge in any environment. But the aquatic environment is particularly challenging for a mammal, which must continually breathe and maintain a constant body temperature in addition to finding prey, avoiding predators, and raising young. Cetaceans have specialized adaptations that enable them to survive and be successful in their aquatic habitats.

A visible breath.

Whales breathe through their blowholes. They hold their breath under water, and begin to exhale just before reaching the surface. They inhale quickly and then close their blowholes before submerging. The visible blow of a whale is not water rising from the blowhole, but water vapor from the respiratory gasses condensing in the relatively cooler air. In addition, the whale's forceful exhalation may cause water on top of the blowhole to be atomized into tiny droplets. Some baleen whales can be identified from a distance by the size and shape of their blows. A blue whale's blow can reach 9 m (30 ft.) straight up into the air; a gray whale's blow may appear heart-shaped when seen from behind; and a right whale's blow is v-shaped. Sperm whales also have a distinctive blow that angles forward and to the left.

Whale respiration patterns differ depending on the species and activity. For example, traveling gray whales usually dive for 3 to 5 minutes, then surface and blow three to five times at 15 to 30 second intervals before diving again. In contrast, sperm whales rest in place at the surface for about 8 minutes in between lengthy, foraging dives.

Toothed whales exchange 80%, and baleen whales exchange 80% to 90% of their lung air volume with each respiration, making them very efficient breathers. Humans only exchange about 17% of their lung air.

Swift swimmers.

All whales move with up-and-down movements of the tail flukes. The flukes are powered by muscle masses in the upper and lower regions of the *tail stock*. Pectoral flippers help the whale to steer and, with the help of the flukes, to stop.

Because of their size, baleen whales are generally slow swimmers. Migrating gray whales swim about 4.5 to 9 kph (2.8–5.6 mph). Rorquals, which are more streamlined than other mysticete families, are known for reaching speeds of more than 36 kph (22 mph)—the fastest for baleen whales. Toothed whales are typically faster swimmers than baleen whales. One of the fastest whales is the killer whale, which can reach speeds of 45 kph (28 mph) for short distances. Ganges and Indus river dolphins generally swim slowly. For these dolphins, a burst speed is about 5.4 kph (3 mph).

At high swim speeds, some fast-swimming toothed whales *porpoise* at the surface: they swim fast enough to break free of the water, flying up and out and then back under in one continuous movement, which they generally repeat. Porpoising uses less energy than swimming fast at the surface. Certain toothed whales, such as common and bottlenose dolphins, sometimes ride ocean swells or a boat's bow or stern wake. Riding a wave or a wake, a dolphin can go almost twice as fast using the same energy cost.

Blue whales have a tall, columnar blow. Photo by Patricia Schick.

Special physiological adaptations help sperm whales conserve oxygen when t dive to depths greater than 1,000 m (3,281 ft.). Photo by Flip Nicklin, Minden Pictures.

Diving deep.

Whales are champion divers, far exceeding the best human freedivers (diving without air) in both time and depth. Champion human freedivers can hold their breath for more than two minutes during an actual dive—well beyond the abilities of most humans. In 2005, the human record for an assisted freedive was to 172 m (564 ft.). Whales and other marine mammals regularly exceed these human dive limits. Like all marine mammals, whales have special physiological adaptations that help them conserve and effectively utilize oxygen during a dive. When an animal dives, its heart rate automatically slows and blood is shunted away from tissue that is more tolerant of lower oxygen levels, and concentrated in the heart, lungs, and brain where oxygen is needed most. In addition, whales store more oxygen for use during deep dives. Pound for pound, whales have twice the concentration of *hemoglobin* and up to nine times the concentration of *myoglobin* of terrestrial animals. Like hemoglobin, myoglobin—found in muscle tissue—is an oxygen-binding protein.

Toothed and baleen whales that roam and forage in shallow, coastal waters do not regularly dive to extreme depths for long lengths of time. Yet, many oceanic species of toothed whales surpass all other mammals with their diving abilities. Sperm whales are champion deep divers. About 99.5% of their dives are to depths 1,000 m (3,281 ft.) or less. Yet, they are capable of diving even deeper: sonar tracking has detected sperm whales deeper than 2,250 m (7,382 ft. or 1.4 miles). For sperm whales, dives lasting 60 to 90 minutes are common. Members of the beaked whale family also are known for deep diving. For both Cuvier's beaked whales and northern bottlenose whales, dives to depths of 1,450 m (4,757 ft.) and for as long as 90 minutes have been documented. Not surprisingly, most beaked whales and sperm whales routinely dive deep to primarily prey on deepwater squid.

Unlike human divers, whales don't get "the bends" (decompression sickness) when they dive. When humans dive with air tanks, decompression sickness can result from changes in the state of nitrogen molecules (the largest component of air) inside the body following changes in pressure. This occurs because nitrogen becomes more soluble as pressure increases. As a human diver ascends, dissolved nitrogen returns to its gaseous state and tiny bubbles may form inside the capillaries (the tiniest blood vessels). Because it breathes at the surface, a whale isn't inhaling air under pressure. As a whale dives deeply its flexible lungs collapse forcing air into the windpipe and nasal ducts where internal body surfaces can't absorb nitrogen. In addition, following deep, prolonged dives, deep-diving whales such as beaked whales slow their ascent and spend more time resting at the surface to give their tissues a chance to offload excess nitrogen. Other research suggests that the slowing of the heart rate during a dive and increase as the whale begins to surface may also reduce the amount of nitrogen in a whale's bloodstream. Nevertheless, after repeated dives, the nitrogen concentration in a toothed whale's muscle tissue may build up. Under experimental conditions, researchers measured the nitrogen concentration in a bottlenose dolphin's muscle after the dolphin made repeated dives to about 50 m (164 ft.). They found a nitrogen concentration high enough to cause decompression sickness in humans. This experiment suggests that cetaceans can tolerate higher nitrogen concentrations than humans, although further study is needed on how cetaceans tolerate these higher nitrogen loads.

Thermoregulation.

Heat loss in water is about 25 times faster than in air at the same temperature. Despite this incredible rate of heat loss, whales maintain a core body temperature somewhere between 36°C to 37°C (96.8–98.6°F). This temperature is similar to that of other large mammals.

How do whales regulate their body temperature? First of all, whales deposit most of their body fat into a thick insulating *blubber* layer just underneath the skin. Blubber is composed of fat cells within a matrix of collagen—a type of fibrous connective tissue.

A countercurrent heat exchange system in the flippers, flukes, and dorsal fin helps a whale maintain its body temperature. Pictured is a killer whale (top) extending a pectoral flipper out of the water and the flukes of a humpback whale (bottom: photo by Patricia Schick.)

Heat from the blood traveling through the arteries is transferred to the blood traveling through the veins, and is carried back to the body core, rather than being lost to the environment.

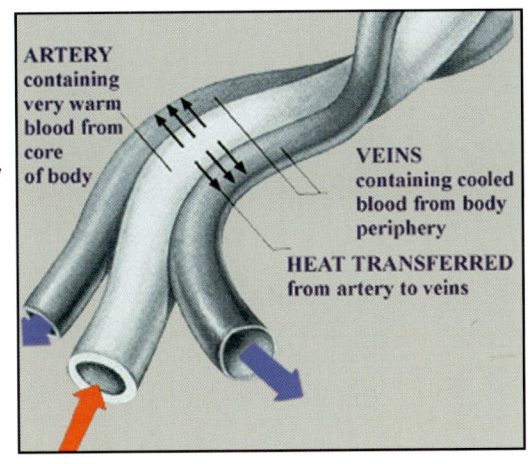

ARTERY containing very warm blood from core of body

VEINS containing cooled blood from body periphery

HEAT TRANSFERRED from artery to veins

Blubber insulates a whale and slows heat loss in the cold ocean water. There is a decreasing heat gradient throughout the blubber to the skin, which is only a degree or two above that of the surrounding water. The blubber layer can reach a thickness of 50 cm (20 in.) on a bowhead whale. Blubber also gives a whale its fusiform body shape, making it streamlined and allowing energy-efficient swimming. In addition, blubber acts as an energy reserve when a whale's food intake is reduced.

In addition to having an insulating blubber layer, the large size of baleen whales and many toothed whales helps minimize heat loss. In general, as an animal increases in size, its surface area decreases relative to volume. A whale's fusiform body shape and reduced limb size further decrease this surface-to-volume ratio. A low surface-to-volume ratio helps an animal retain body heat; the large body core produces metabolic heat. Only through the relatively smaller surface area exposed to the external environment (the skin) is that heat lost.

A whale's circulatory system adjusts to conserve or dissipate body heat and maintain body temperature. Some arteries of the flippers, flukes, and dorsal fin are surrounded by veins. Thus, some heat from the blood traveling through arteries is transferred to venous blood rather than the environment. This phenomenon is called *countercurrent heat exchange*. When a whale dives, circulation decreases at the skin, shunting blood to the insulated body core. During prolonged exercise or in warm water a whale may need to dissipate body heat. In this case, circulation increases near the surface of the body, flippers, flukes, and dorsal fin and excess heat is shed to the external environment.

Whale Behavior

"Some of the subtlest secrets of the seas seemed divulged to us in this enchanted pond. ...And thus, though surrounded by circle upon circle of consternation and affrights, did these inscrutable creatures... freely and fearlessly indulge in all peaceful concernments; yea, serenely revelled in dalliance and delight."

from **Moby Dick** by Herman Melville

Many dolphins, such as bottlenose dolphins, live in fluid social groups.

What Whales Do

Individual whale behaviors depend on the species and, to some extent, the size of the whale. Many species of whales often *breach*—a behavior in which a whale powerfully thrusts a large part of its body out of the water and lands on the surface—usually on its side or on its back—with a huge splash. Often the same whale will breach several times in sequence. Some species, such as humpback whales, sperm whales and various species of dolphins, frequently breach while other whales, like blue whales, most beaked whales, river dolphins, and porpoises rarely breach. Although, the function of breaching in whales remains a mystery, many researchers believe, that in some cases, whales breach as a signal to other whales of the same species or to dislodge external parasites.

In addition to breaching, other individual behaviors commonly seen in whales include *lobtailing*, *pec-slapping*, and *spyhopping*. Lobtailing (slapping the tail flukes on the surface of the water) and pec-slapping (slapping a pectoral flipper on the surface of the water) create loud sounds above water and under water. These two behaviors probably function in communication. A spyhop is when a whale rises out of the water somewhat vertically, exposing its head. A spyhopping whale often slowly turns around to scan the area.

Some dolphin species, such as striped dolphins, Pacific white-sided dolphins, and dusky dolphins are known for their aerial acrobatics. Spinner dolphins are named for their characteristic behavior of leaping from the water and spinning vertically in mid-air. Many dolphin species and other small toothed whales often ride the bow waves of boats or even of sperm whales or large baleen whales. Sheer mass limits the physical behaviors of most baleen whales. Due to their enormous size, blue whales rarely leap or breach. Yet, humpbacks are among the most acrobatic of baleen whales.

Individual behaviors include (clockwise from the top) breaching (killer whale), spyhopping (gray whale), and lobtailing (humpback whale: photo by Patricia Schick.)

Like most toothed whales, common dolphins are highly social. Group size ranges from less than ten to hundreds or even thousands of dolphins.

Social behavior.

Most species of toothed whales are highly social animals that live in groups. Bottlenose dolphins live in fluid social groups. Some toothed whales, such as killer whales, live in cohesive social units called *pods*. Killer whale pods usually consist of related animals of both sexes with very close bonds between the females. Sperm whales generally group themselves into one of three kinds of pods: nursery pods made up of females and calves, bachelor pods consisting of young males, and pods made up entirely of mature males. Most pods seem to exhibit some social hierarchy. In whales, either males or females are dominant, depending on the species.

The number of animals in a pod varies according to the species and the pod. Several pods may occasionally join to form a *herd*. Certain species, such as melon-headed whales, common dolphins, and dusky dolphins, have been seen in large herds of more than 1,000 individuals. When the herd splits up again, there may be an exchange of some pod members.

Social behaviors in toothed whales are numerous and varied. Social interactions may include tail-slapping, head-butting, jaw-snapping, chasing and charging, and bubble-blowing. Toothed whales of many species commonly rake or scratch one another with their teeth. Such interactions may be for competition or to establish dominance. Researchers theorize that male beaked whales use their teeth only for establishing dominance and for displays of aggression and competition, not for feeding. Raking leaves superficial lacerations that soon heal, although traces of light parallel stripes often remain on the skin.

In contrast to most toothed whale species, baleen whales are often found singly or in loose associations rather than in large groups or families. Migrating baleen whales may swim in small groups, and some species mate in groups. Large numbers may congregate in feeding or calving areas. The strongest apparent bond among individual baleen whales is between a calf and its mother.

Sound production.

Whales rely on sound production and reception to communicate, navigate, and hunt, especially when dark and murky conditions render vision almost useless. Under water, where sound waves travel about 4.5 times faster than in air, vocal communication is very effective.

Baleen whales tend to be more solitary than toothed whales. The closest bond is between a mother and her calf. Pictured is a gray whale calf (foreground) and cow (background). Photo by Patricia Schick.

All whales lack vocal cords. In baleen whales, the origin of sounds is not fully understood, but researchers suspect that the larynx is responsible. Much more is known about sound production in odontocetes. A toothed whale makes pulse sounds by moving air between nasal sacs in the blowhole region. It has a tissue complex in the nasal region under the blowhole that is the site of sound production. In most toothed whales, this complex includes two sets of *phonic lips*—sound-producing structures that project into the nasal passage. A sperm whale has just one set of phonic lips. Toothed whales make at least some sounds by forcing air through the nasal passage and past the phonic lips. The surrounding tissue vibrates, producing sound.

A toothed whale's melon acts as an acoustical lens to focus and direct sound waves into a beam that is projected forward into the water in front of the whale. In sperm whales, which lack a melon, at least some sound probably travels directly out into the water in front of the whale, but some sound probably reverberates through the spermaceti organ and the junk before traveling away from the whale. Some scientists have theorized that the sound travels backward though the spermaceti and then forward through the junk. In this scenario, the junk focuses the sound into a beam, as does the melon of other toothed whales.

Killer whale vocalizations have been studied extensively at Hubbs-SeaWorld Research Institute.

The repertoire of baleen whale sounds includes very low-frequency (20–200 Hz) moans, grunts, thumps and knocks; and higher-frequency (above 1000 Hz) chirps, cries, and whistles. Baleen whale sounds may be the loudest produced by any animal and may travel tens or even hundreds of kilometers under water. Types of vocalizations vary by species.

The frequency of sounds that toothed whales make depends on the species. Various toothed whale sounds have been recorded at frequencies ranging from 5 kHz to more than 135 kHz. For most species, lower frequency vocalizations probably function mainly in communication, and higher frequency clicks, in echolocation. As a group, odontocetes produce sounds that resemble moans, groans, trills, grunts, squeaks, creaks, cracks, squawks, snaps, and barks. These sounds vary by species in volume, frequency, duration, and pattern and probably function in social interactions. Toothed whales also produce broadband clicks for echolocation. Many species of odontocetes also produce whistles. Whistles last a half-second to a few seconds and probably are social sounds. There is some evidence that individual bottlenose dolphins make unique signature whistles.

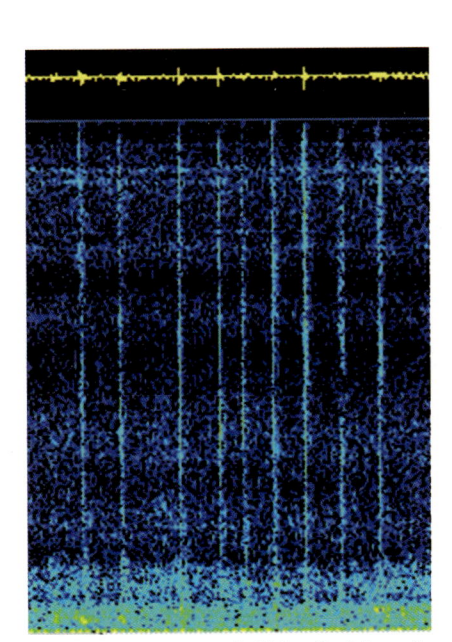

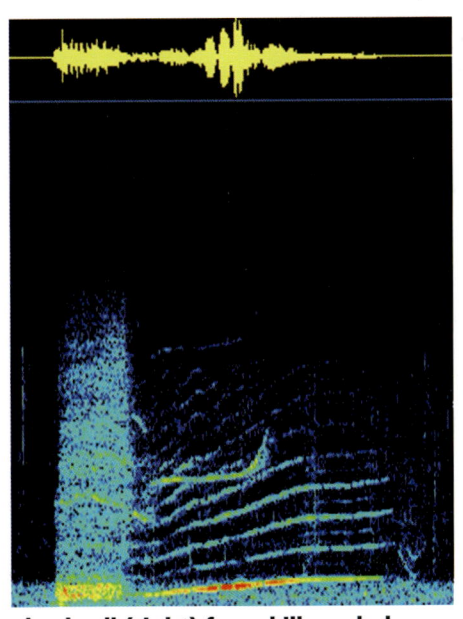

Spectrograms of clicks (left) and a pulsed call (right) from killer whales studied by scientists at Hubbs-SeaWorld Research Institute.

Communication.

Whales probably vocalize to communicate information regarding orientation, greeting, aggression, individual recognition, or breeding readiness.

Among baleen whales, humpback whales are probably the most vocal. When in breeding grounds, mature male humpback whales produce a series of repeating units of sounds (up to 8,000 Hz) that are classified as "songs." Experts speculate that such vocalizations—which can last more than 30 minutes—may keep males spaced apart; attract females; make it possible for whales to locate each other; or communicate information such as species, sex, location, mate status, and readiness to compete with other males for mates. Further study is necessary to determine the true function of these songs.

Toothed whales, which are more social than baleen whales, communicate with each other on a regular basis. But there is no evidence that any species of toothed whale has anything resembling human language.

Researchers have studied killer whale vocals extensively both in the wild and in zoological parks such as SeaWorld. Killer whale calls that sound the same time after time are called *stereotyped calls*. All a killer whale's stereotyped calls make up that whale's *repertoire*. The individuals of any particular pod share the same repertoire of calls, a vocalization system called a *dialect*. Although scientists have noted that there is some type of structure to the calls, a dialect is not the same thing as a language. Analysis of killer whale call patterns has demonstrated substantial differences between the dialects of different pods.

Pods that associate with one another may share certain calls. Pods that share calls are called a *clan*. No two pods share an entire repertoire—each pod has its own unique dialect. In fact, the vocal repertoires of each pod remain distinct enough that scientists can identify pods by the sounds they make. Killer whales that are separated by great geographical distances have completely different dialects. An analysis of Icelandic and Norwegian killer whale pods revealed that the Icelandic population made 24 different calls and the Norwegian whales made 23 different calls, but the two populations did not share any of the same calls. Vocal development studies at SeaWorld have indicated that a calf learns its repertoire of calls selectively from its mother even when other killer whales may be present and vocalize more frequently than the mother.

When socializing, sperm whales produce rhythmic patterns of clicks called *codas*. Some individuals produce unique codas, while other codas are shared by several whales in local groups. Codas may allow individuals or groups to recognize or locate one another. Some researchers suggest that sperm whales can also be categorized into acoustic clans.

Like many other animals, whales may also communicate using a variety of postures and gestures. Some behaviors, such as head-butting and jaw-snapping, are usually assumed to communicate aggression. The purpose of other behaviors, including breaching and pec-slapping, is not clearly understood.

Echolocation.

Echolocation is the ability of toothed whales (and most bats) to locate and discriminate objects by producing high-frequency sound waves, and receiving and interpreting the resulting echoes. Toothed whales produce directional, broad band clicks in trains. Each click lasts less than a thousandth of a second. The click train passes through the melon (the rounded, fatty region of the forehead). The melon probably functions as an acoustic lens to focus the sound waves into a beam, which is projected forward through the water in front of the whale. The sound waves travel through water at a speed of about 1.5 km per second (0.9 mi./sec). They bounce off objects in the water and return to the whale in the form of an echo.

With the help of echolocation, toothed whales—like pilot whales—can determine the size, shape, and distance of objects in the water.

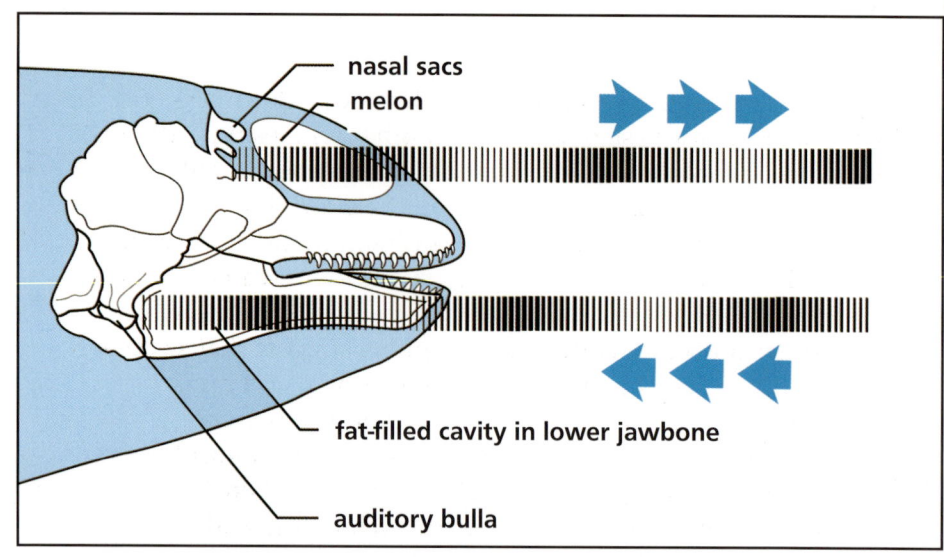

Diagram labels: nasal sacs, melon, fat-filled cavity in lower jawbone, auditory bulla

Toothed whales echolocate by producing and sending high-frequency clicks, and receiving and interpreting the resulting echoes.

The whale probably receives the echoes through the fat-filled cavities of the lower jawbones. Sounds are conducted through the lower jaw to the middle ear, inner ear, and then through the auditory nerve to hearing centers in the brain. The brain receives the sound waves in the form of nerve impulses, which relay the message of the sound and enable the whale to interpret the sound's meaning. Because high-frequency sounds don't travel as far through water as low-frequency sounds, echolocation is most effective at close to intermediate range—about 5 to 200 m (16–656 ft.) for targets 5 to 15 cm (2–6 in.) in length.

By this complex system, toothed whales can determine the size, shape, distance, velocity, and even some degree of internal structure of objects in the water. Through repeated experience, bottlenose dolphins learn and later recognize the echo signatures of preferred prey species. The deep-foraging sperm whales are long-distance echolocators. Theoretical calculations suggest that they can detect the sea floor and prey from as far away as 16 km (10 miles).

There is no evidence that indicates baleen whales echolocate as toothed whales do. Studies have shown, however, that bowhead whales produce low-frequency sounds that may give the whales information about the ocean floor and locations of ice floes and ice sheets.

Do whales sleep?

Sleep in cetaceans is not yet clearly understood. Observers note that killer whales, bottlenose dolphins, and other whales typically rest motionless at various times throughout the day and night. A preliminary study looking at SeaWorld Orlando's killer whales, suggests that they spend nearly half (44.5%) of their time resting, either at the surface or at the bottom. In addition, studies on gray whales, bottlenose dolphins, belugas, boto, pilot whales, harbor porpoises, and Pacific white-sided dolphins suggest that sleep in whales probably occurs in one brain hemisphere at a time. Furthermore, studies indicate that whales only experience slow-wave or non-rapid-eye-movement sleep. Unihemispheric slow-wave sleep may be an aquatic adaptation that enables a whale to monitor its environment, keep swimming, and control respiration.

Additional studies indicate different rest patterns for cetacean mothers with new calves. Sleep researchers studied two bottlenose dolphin mother-calf pairs and two killer whale mother-calf pairs at SeaWorld San Diego. They discovered that the mothers and calves didn't appear to sleep or rest at all for the first month of a calf's life. Over the next several months, the whales gradually increased the amount of time they spent resting to normal adult levels. Staying active and responsive after birth may be an adaptation for avoiding predators and maintaining body temperature while the calf builds up a layer of blubber.

Studies on a number of whale species suggest that sleep in whales occurs in one brain hemisphere at a time.

Killer whales in Antarctica spyhop through a hole in the ice for a look at emperor and Adélie penguins. Photo by Paul Ponganis.

Food and Foraging.

For the most part, baleen and toothed whales exhibit different food preferences. Baleen whales forage low on the food chain—primarily eating zooplankton (tiny drifting animals) and small schooling fishes. The specialized filter-feeding design of a baleen whale's head and mouth enable it to consume large quantities of these minute organisms that often occur in swarms or schools. Probably the most common source of food for the baleen whales is *krill*—a shrimplike crustacean, about 2.6 cm (1 in.) long. Millions of krill form large swarms. Unlike other baleen whales, gray whales feed mainly on benthic (bottom-dwelling) organisms such as shrimplike *amphipods* and marine worms.

Toothed whales feed mostly on various fishes and squids, although some also eat shrimps and other crustaceans. Some populations of killer whales prey on marine mammals and seabirds such as penguins. Because members of the same species may inhabit different geographical areas, food preferences and resources often vary with location.

In the northeastern Pacific and some other areas, overlapping populations of killer whales show very different foraging patterns. The transient form of killer whale preys on a variety of marine mammals including seals, sea lions, other toothed whales, baleen whales, and occasionally sea otters. Resident killer whales eat only fish. A less-studied, offshore form of killer whale probably only eats fishes and squids. Killer whales in Antarctic waters exhibit similar prey variance. "Type A" whales eat mostly Antarctic minke whales. "Type B" whales eat mainly seals, but also prey on minke and humpback whales. "Type C" killer whales eat mostly Antarctic toothfish (*Dissostichus mawsoni*).

Whales consume an average of 4% to 6% of their body weight in food daily, but this amount may range (with species) from 1% to 12%. The amount an individual consumes increases during growth spurts, nursing, and other demanding physiological processes. Most baleen whales spend about four to six months in the summer feeding intensively in high-latitude productive waters, in preparation for the next six to eight months they will spend migrating and breeding. During this feeding period, food intake exceeds daily requirements, and excess energy is stored in the blubber layer. This energy reserve sustains the whale during the winter months, when it is engaged in activities other than feeding.

Catching a meal.

Foraging behavior is the main area that separates toothed whales from baleen whales. Most toothed whales use their teeth for grasping and tearing food, while baleen whales are filter feeders.

All baleen whales use their baleen to strain food from the water, but demonstrate different feeding styles. Right whales, including bowheads, continuously skim the surface for zooplankton such as copepods as they swim near or at the surface with mouth open. Water and food enter the open mouth through gaps between baleen plates. Food is caught on the matted baleen fringes inside, and water exits through the sides of the mouth.

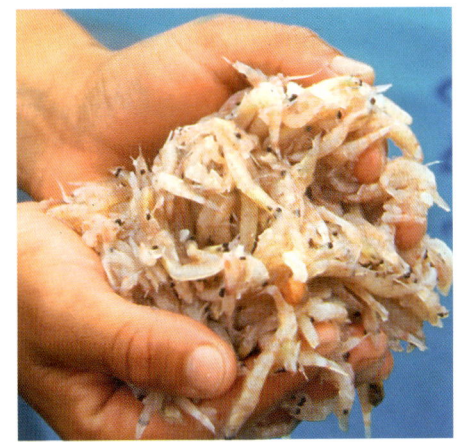

Krill—tiny shrimplike crustaceans— are a staple for many baleen whales.

Bottom-feeding gray whales in the Arctic trail flumes of mud behind them.

Rorquals vary in their feeding habits. They often gulp large quantities of crustaceans and schooling fishes, allowing both food and water to enter the mouth. The rostrum is usually tilted upward. Throat grooves expand from the water pressure inside, which causes the mouth cavity to balloon out, greatly increasing its capacity. The jaws are brought together and the throat grooves contract, forcing water to drain out the sides of the mouth.

Unlike other baleen whales, gray whales typically forage along the ocean floor. Turning on its side, a gray whale sucks in water, silt, and benthic animals. The baleen traps food and lets water and mud escape. Scientists have observed gray whales surfacing after feeding, trailing flumes of mud behind them. Bowhead whales also occasionally feed at or near the bottom, although observers have found no evidence that bowheads suction feed off the bottom like gray whales.

Whales mostly hunt individually, but many toothed whales and some baleen whales hunt cooperatively to obtain prey. In open waters, some dolphins such as bottlenose dolphins, often feed cooperatively with other group members. They encircle and herd a

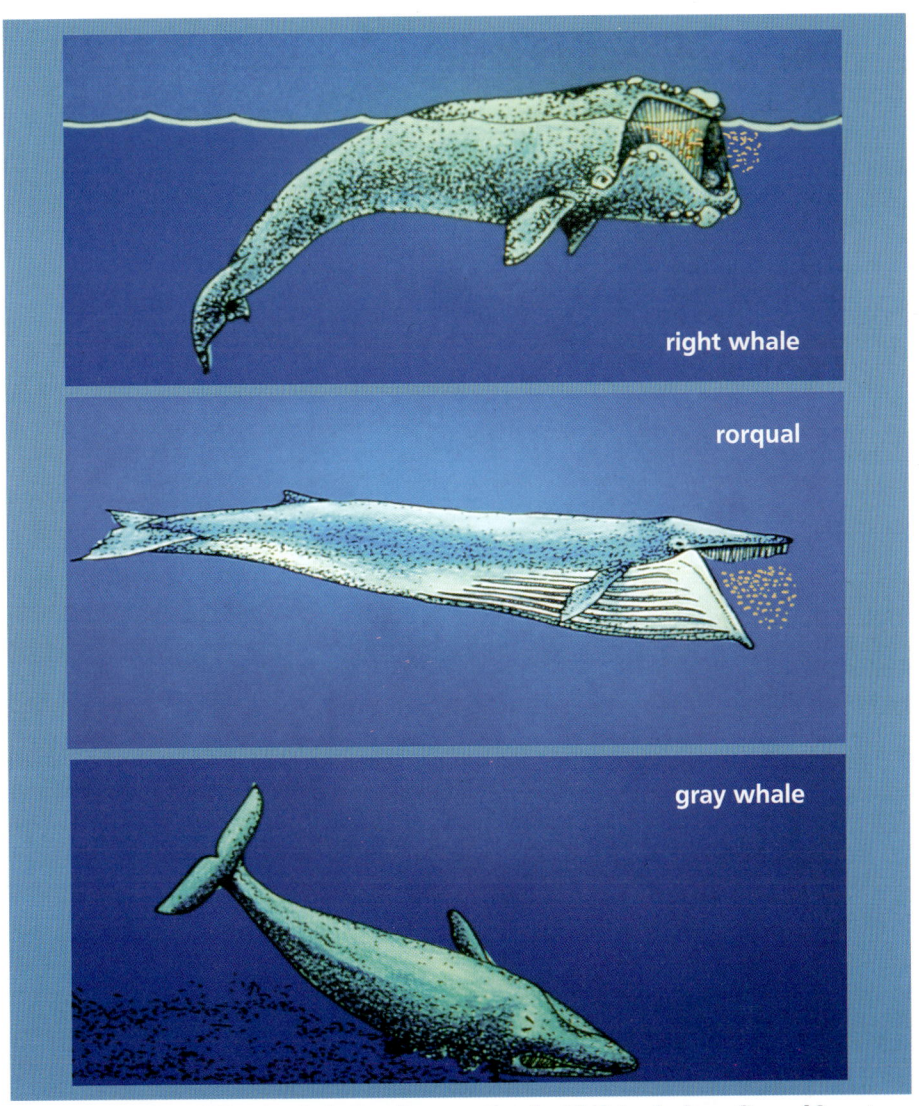

Baleen whales differ in their feeding methods. Right whales often skim at the surface; rorquals typically lunge feed; and gray whales usually scoop up huge mouthfuls of mud containing amphipods and other marine animals from the ocean bottoms.

large school of fish into a dense mass, then take turns charging through the school to feed. Occasionally, individual dolphins herd fish to shallow water and trap them against a shore or sandbar. In Patagonia, killer whales sometimes purposely strand to catch elephant seal or sea lion pups in the surf zone and then rock sideways to catch a wave back into deeper water. Humpback whales sometimes feed cooperatively in a method called bubble netting to help them gather schooling fish.

Species Spotlights

"The whales turn and glisten, plunge and sound and rise again,

Hanging over subtly darkening deeps

Flowing like breathing planets in the sparkling whorls of living light—"

Gary Snyder

Bowhead Whale
Balaena mysticetus

Bowhead whales are members of the right whale family. Photo by Andries Blouw (Fisheries and Oceans Canada).

Bowhead whales are named for the bowed line of their mouth, which holds the longest baleen—up to 4.3 m (14 ft.)—of any mysticete whale. Like the other members of the right whale family, bowheads reach lengths of 18 m (59 ft.) for males and 20 m (66 ft.) for females. They usually weigh 68,039 to 90,718 kg (75–100 tons). Bowheads are mostly black with a white chin and white on the tail stock and flukes. They are sometimes white or gray on other parts of the body. Adults may have completely white flukes.

Bowheads live only in the arctic and subarctic regions in close association with the pack ice. Their migration coincides with the formation of the ice. They travel to the high latitudes in summer as the ice recedes, and then follow the developing ice edge southward in winter. Bowheads can dive for up to an hour when traveling under ice sheets and use their massive heads to break through ice up to 1.8 m (6 in.) thick.

Bowheads produce loud, low frequency calls, particularly during migration and in the breeding season. These calls may help bowheads keep in contact when navigating under sea ice and are used to attract mates. In addition, mature male bowheads produce songlike vocalizations in the spring, possibly to attract females. Bowheads frequently breach and lobtail, behaviors that may play a role in mate attraction or in asserting dominance.

When feeding, bowheads usually skim at the surface for copepods, krill, and other planktonic prey. They also occasionally forage along the seafloor for other prey such as amphipods. Bowheads typically feed alone. However, sometimes up to 12 bowheads will coordinate their behavior and feed in an *echelon* (inverted v-shaped) formation.

As with other right whales, 16th to 19th century commercial whalers hunted bowheads nearly to extinction. Whalers targeted bowheads primarily for their extremely long plates of baleen for use in many common items of the time including dress hoops, corset stays, umbrella ribs, and buggy whips. Whalers also rendered bowhead blubber into whale oil, popular at the time for a variety of everyday uses.

Bowhead whales live in close association with the ice. Photo by Andries Blouw (Fisheries and Oceans Canada).

Blue Whale
Balaenoptera musculus

Blue whales are named for their blue-gray coloration. Photo by Patricia Schick

The blue whale is the largest animal on Earth. These behemoths wander throughout the world's oceans. Long ago, Antarctic blue whales measured more than 30.5 m (100 ft.) and weighed up to 145,280 kg (160,000 tons), before whale hunters took the most massive individuals. The largest blue whales today measure about 27 m (89 ft.), but lengths of 23 m (75 ft.) are more common. Blue whales generally weigh between 72,575 to 136,078 kg. (80–150 tons). Southern hemisphere blues tend to grow larger than their northern counterparts.

Blue whales, named for their mottled bluish-gray color, can be glimpsed when they surface to breathe. A blue whale's slender, vertical blow reaches heights of 10 m (33 ft.) or more. The relatively tiny dorsal fin of a blue whale lies far back on the body, appearing well after the whale surfaces. Blue whales occasionally fluke before a dive, however not as often as humpbacks or gray whales.

These giant whales mainly eat krill, but occasionally consume pelagic crabs when available. The largest blue whales may eat up to

5,443 kg (6 tons) of krill each day. They typically feed alone or in pairs, although aggregations of up to 50 blues sometimes feed in areas with abundant, clustered prey.

Blue whales produce the loudest calls (up to 188 decibels) of any animal. Their low frequency calls of 17 to 20 Hz remain below the human hearing range. Yet other blue whales probably detect these calls hundreds to thousands of kilometers away. These sounds may be used for communication or in navigation.

Females give birth to a single calf every two or three years following a 12-month gestation. Blue whale calves measure about 7 m (23 ft.) and 2,700 to 3,600 kg (6,000–8,000 lb.). Calves are weaned at six to eight months, when they gain as much as 90 kg (200 lb.) a day.

Widespread commercial whaling during the 19th and early 20th centuries severely depleted blue whale populations. The worldwide population is currently about 10,000 to 14,000, a fraction of the more than 200,000 blue whales that once roamed the seas. Blue whales are protected by several U.S. and international treaties and agencies, including the International Whaling Commission, the U.S. Marine Mammal Protection Act of 1972, and the U.S. Endangered Species Act of 1973. But despite more than 50 years of protection, blue whale populations have not recovered.

A blue whale's flukes are sometimes raised above the water before a dive.

Humpback Whale
Megaptera novaeangliae

Humpbacks often arch before diving—emphasizing their humps and tiny dorsal fins. Photo by Patricia Schick.

Humpback whales are mostly black with white on the belly, flippers and flukes. The pectoral flippers are extremely long—up to one third of the whale's body length. Like fingerprints, the humpback's flukes are unique to each individual whale and range in color from all white, to mottled black and white, to all black on the underside. As with most other baleen whales, female humpbacks grow larger than males; averaging lengths of about 14 to 15 m (46–50 ft.). Males grow to approximately 12.5 to 14 m (41–50 ft.).

Humpback whales inhabit all oceans and migrate thousands of miles between higher latitude summer feeding grounds to winter breeding grounds in the tropics. They are amazing acrobats—often breaching or slapping their flukes or flippers on the water.

Humpback whales are one of the most vocal baleen whales. They produce a series of repeating sounds called "songs" that can last more than 30 minutes. Adult males typically sing while in the breeding grounds. Although scientists do not know why humpback whales sing, the songs probably play a role in reproduction.

Humpbacks sometimes blow "bubble nets" to help them gather fish. One member of a foraging group dives down, and then swims up toward the surface in a slow spiral while releasing a series of tiny bubbles from the blowholes. The bubbles form a tubular "net" confusing and trapping schooling fishes. The whales then surface in the center with their mouths open to engulf the trapped prey.

Due to extensive hunting by 19th and early 20th century whalers, humpback whale populations were severely depleted. Although populations have slightly recovered, humpback whales are listed as "endangered" on the U.S. Endangered Species List and are protected by several other national and international laws.

Humpbacks are highly acrobatic—they frequently lunge forward out of the water (top) and breach (bottom). Photos by Patricia Schick.

Gray Whale
Eschrichtius robustus

Gray whales are named for their mottled gray coloration. Photo by Patricia Schick

The gray whale is the only species in the baleen whale family Eschrichtiidae. The California population of gray whales is found in the eastern North Pacific off the western coast of North America. A second, extremely rare population of gray whales lives in the western North Pacific along the coast of Asia. While the eastern North Pacific gray whale population is well-studied, little is known about the critically endangered western North Pacific population. Researchers believe their behavior is probably similar to the California gray whale's behavior.

As its name implies, the gray whale has a gray body mottled with lighter patches—mainly from encrusting barnacles and whale lice or scars from previous infestations of these parasites. Unlike other baleen whales with numerous throat pleats, the gray whale has only two to seven throat grooves. Instead of a dorsal fin, the gray whale has a dorsal hump followed by a set of eight to fourteen small knuckles along the tail stock. Mature female gray whales average 14.1 m (46 ft.) in length. Male gray whales are generally smaller, averaging 13 m (43 ft.). Adult gray whales weigh 16,000 to 45,000 kg (35,274–99,208 lb.).

California gray whales may migrate farther than any other marine mammal. They journey between feeding and breeding grounds and cross national and international borders. Grays spend the summers feasting on marine invertebrates—especially amphipods that they scoop up and strain from the muddy bottoms of the Bering and Chukchi Seas. Some gray whales also opportunistically surface skim or engulf planktonic prey in different locations along the North Pacific coast. Most gray whales migrate south in the fall as the ice pack starts to form. The whales swim along the North American coastline to breeding lagoons in Baja California, Mexico—a distance of up to 10,000 kilometers (6,214 miles). The first wave of migration consists of near-term pregnant females, followed by estrus females and mature males, followed by immature males and females. In the warm, shallow waters of Laguna Ojo de Liebre (Scammon's Lagoon), Laguna Guerro Negro (Black Warrior Lagoon), Laguna San Ignacio, and Magdalena Bay, some gray whales mate and mothers care for their 4.6 to 4.9 m (15–16 ft.) newborn calves. After a few months, the gray whales travel back up north to the Alaskan Arctic with the mother-calf pairs leaving last. The calves remain with their mothers for six to seven months until they are weaned on the feeding grounds in the summer.

During the 19th and early 20th centuries, whalers hunted gray whales to the brink of extinction. After a ban on hunting in 1946, the population of California gray whales began to recover. Scientists believe that the current population is close to pre-whaling numbers. In 1994, the California gray whale was the first marine mammal removed from the U.S. Endangered Species List. In contrast, the western North Pacific population, which is estimated at only about 100 whales, remains listed as "endangered" on the U.S. Endangered Species List and as "critically endangered" on the IUCN's Redlist.

A gray whale breaches in Laguna San Ignacio. Photo by Patricia Schick

Sperm Whale
Physeter macrocephalus

The distinctive blow of a sperm whale angles forward and to the left. Photo by Patricia Schick.

The sperm whale is a huge and highly distinctive toothed whale. Bulls reach lengths of 16 m (52.5 ft.) and may weigh as much as 40,800 kg (114,000 lb.); making these the largest odontocete. Females grow to 12 m (39.4 ft.) in length.

A sperm whale's squarish head is massive—one fourth to one third of its body length. The lower jaw is narrow with 20 to 26 conical teeth that fit into grooves in the upper jaw. The blowhole angles forward and to the left giving the sperm whale a characteristic slanted blow. Although the head is smooth, the rest of the sperm whale's skin is wrinkled. Instead of a dorsal fin, the whale has a rounded dorsal hump followed by a series of bumps on the tail stock. The short, broad pectoral flippers are rounded at the tips and the flukes are triangular with a well-defined median notch.

Sperm whales inhabit the world's oceans. Females tend to remain in temperate and tropic waters while males migrate into higher latitudes. Sperm whales often roam and dive in the deep, offshore waters of underwater canyons—foraging for squid and deepwater fishes.

As commercial whaling depleted the giant baleen whales in the 18th and 19th centuries, more and more commercial fisheries around the world focused on sperm whales. Whalers prized the spermaceti oil from the whale's spermaceti organ and a related tissue called the "junk"—both located in the sperm whale's huge head. Products of sperm whales were used for candles, lamp fuel, soaps, cosmetics, ointments, glue, leather, ink, and animal food. Whalers also valued *ambergris*—a musky scented, waxy substance that forms in the large intestines of some sperm whales, often embedded with squid beaks. In the 16th century, ambergris was highly prized as a fixative for perfumes. During the 20th century, the perfume industry replaced ambergris with synthetic chemicals and commercial sperm whaling ended in the 1980s. Since then, sperm whale populations seem to be recovering in some areas such as Antarctica, yet numbers of sperms whales are still well below pre-whaling numbers in other regions like the southeastern Pacific.

A sperm whale throws its flukes out of the water before it dives. Photo by Patricia Schick.

Cuvier's Beaked Whale
Ziphius cavirostris

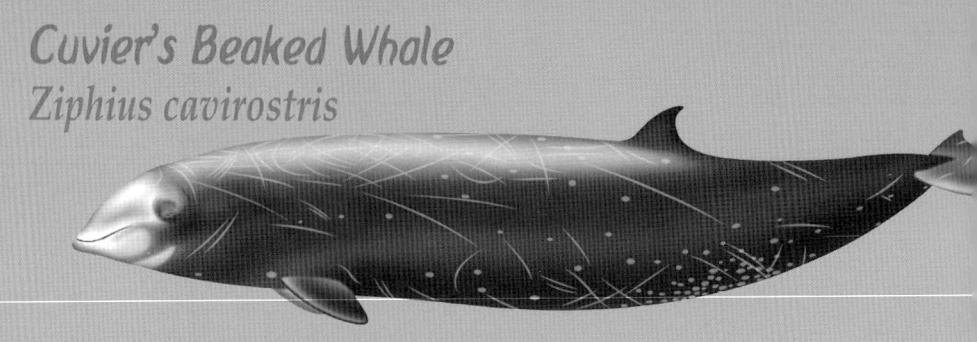

The Cuvier's beaked whale, found in tropical to temperate waters of all oceans, has the widest distribution of any of the beaked whale species. Yet, due to its offshore habitat and frequent diving behavior, it is rarely spotted by humans.

This whale is sometimes called the goose-beaked whale because its short beak and smoothly sloping melon gives this whale a gooselike profile. It reaches maximum lengths of about 7 m (23 ft.). Females, which grow larger, can weigh up to 3,000 kg (6,600 lb.) while males can weigh 2,600 kg (5,700 lb.) or more. Only mature male Cuvier's have two teeth at the tip of their lower jaw—visible even when the whale's mouth is closed. Occasionally, stalked barnacles grow on these exposed teeth. Like most other beaked whales, female Cuvier's have no teeth.

In color, Cuvier's are mostly dark gray to reddish-brown dorsally and lighter on their head and stomach areas. Mature males have mostly white heads—often with a whitish area that extends from the dorsal neck region to the dorsal fin. The skin of adults is frequently marked by scars from cookie cutter sharks or lampreys. Males often have numerous rake marks from the teeth of other males.

Cuvier's beaked whales regularly dive deeply in pursuit of their main prey—deepwater squid. Scientists have recorded Cuvier's diving to depths of 1,450 m (4,757 ft.) and for as long as 90 minutes. Cuvier's also occasionally eat fishes and crustaceans. Like other beaked whales, Cuvier's lack functional teeth and probably catch prey by using suction.

Beaked whale strandings are rare because these deep-diving whales are most likely to die at sea and sink. Most strandings involve a single individual, so any stranding of two or more individuals is classed as a *mass stranding* for these species. Cuvier's beaked whales mass strand more often than any other type of beaked whale. In recent years, a link has been suggested between mass strandings and exposure to underwater sound from high–intensity mid-frequency sonars used in naval defense exercises. A connection between mass strandings and noise from air guns used in seismic exploration has also been suggested; however, the supporting data are not adequate.

Scientists are currently trying to determine the cause of tissue damage found in whales stranded near military exercises using mid-frequency sonars. Some investigators theorize that deep-diving whales may build up substantial concentrations of nitrogen in their tissues while diving repeatedly, and these bubbles could increase in size during exposure to intense sound. If the whales were to surface too rapidly in response to high-intensity sonar, they might get the "bends" and strand as a response to the symptoms. Unfortunately, none of the evidence for these and other theories is strong enough to constitute proof—a different mechanism of injury may be operating. For example, bubbles in tissues of stranded whales have been cited as evidence for the "bends", but bubbles can occur in stranded animals for other reasons. The incidence of bubbles has not yet been studied where there was no exposure to sonar. The appearance of bubbles in strandings associated with sonars may or may not be evidence for an effect. Further research must be conducted before the cause of the strandings can be adequately understood. The U.S. Navy is a major supporter of marine mammal research and is actively working to understand the effects of high-intensity noise, diving patterns of beaked whales, and design of effective mitigation measures, such as using acoustic detection of whales to determine if they are within testing ranges. It also now limits the use of high-intensity sonar in some areas. Scientists hope these measures will help reduce the numbers of mass strandings of Cuvier's beaked whales and other deep-diving cetaceans.

Cuvier's beaked whales often dive deeply to prey on squids. Photo by Tui De Roy (Minden Pictures).

Beluga Whale
Delphinapterus leucas

Beluga whales are sometimes called white whales due to their adult coloration.

Beluga whales are toothed whales in the family Monodontidae. The only other member of this family is the narwhal. Beluga whales inhabit shallow coastal waters of the Arctic Ocean and its adjoining seas including the Sea of Okhotsk, the Bering Sea, the Beaufort Sea, the Gulf of Alaska, Baffin Bay, Hudson Bay, and the Gulf of St. Lawrence. During certain seasons, belugas can even be found in large rivers such as the Amur River of Russia and the Yukon and St. Lawrence Rivers of Canada.

Beluga sizes and weights vary between populations, although males typically grow larger than females. Male belugas in some populations may reach lengths of 5.5 m (18 ft.) while females may grow to 4.1 m (13.4 ft.). Adult belugas at SeaWorld average 3 m (9.8 ft.) in length. Mature males of some beluga stocks can reach weights of about 1,500 kg (3,307 lb.) and females of 1,360 kg (2,998 lb.). Two adult male belugas at SeaWorld average 884 kg (1,948 lb.) in weight, while ten adult females average of 620 kg (1,367 lb.).

Belugas have several adaptations for living in the icy arctic environment. Their white coloration protects belugas from predators by camouflaging them among the icebergs and ice floes of northern seas. At birth, beluga calves are dark gray. A young beluga's skin gradually lightens with age until, by age 13, it attains the white coloration characteristic of adults.

Belugas also lack dorsal fins, and instead, have a low dorsal ridge. Without a dorsal fin, a beluga can more easily swim beneath extensive ice sheets and locate breathing holes. In addition, beluga whales are among the few whales that have unfused neck vertebrae. This makes their necks quite flexible and gives their heads a wide range of motion—increasing their maneuverability while swimming beneath ice sheets and when foraging for bottom-dwelling animals such as octopus, squids, crabs, snails, sandworms, and fishes.

Beluga whales are extremely vocal. Long ago, scientists and sailors called belugas "sea canaries," due to the birdlike sounds these whales make. Many different beluga vocalizations have been recorded including high-pitched whistles and squeals, clucks, mews, chirps, trills, and bell-like tones. Belugas also produce echolocation clicks. They rely on sound to navigate, communicate, locate breathing holes, and hunt in dark or murky waters.

Beluga whales face a number of environmental threats and some populations are declining. Belugas are hunted by subsistence hunters, rather than for commercial use, in Alaska, Canada, Russia, and West Greenland. Environmental contaminants also affect beluga populations. Industrial run-off in the St. Lawrence River has resulted in high levels of PCBs, heavy metals, and other toxins in the water. Many of these toxins become concentrated as they pass up the food chain. Some scientists believe that the deaths, strandings, and low reproductive rates of many belugas are linked to environmental toxins. Major clean-up efforts of the St. Lawrence River may help preserve the local beluga population, yet significant changes may take decades to measure.

A beluga can purse its lips and squirt a stream of water. This may help to dislodge prey from rocks or crevices.

Bottlenose Dolphin
Tursiops truncatus

The coastal ecotype of bottlenose dolphin inhabits harbors, estuaries, lagoons, bays, and other nearshore habitats.

The bottlenose dolphin is the most commonly seen cetacean both in the wild and in zoological parks and aquariums. They inhabit temperate and tropical waters worldwide and live in a variety of habitats from coastal waters to the open ocean. A second species of bottlenose dolphin, *Tursiops aduncus*, ranges throughout the Indo-Pacific.

A bottlenose dolphin is countershaded with a gray to dark gray back that fades to white on its lower jaw and belly. They vary greatly in size ranging from 2 to 3.9 m (6.6–12.8 ft.) in length and averaging 150 to 200 kg (331.5–442 lb.) in weight. Differences in size may be related to variances between coastal and offshore forms and geographical locations. Offshore bottlenose tend to be larger than inshore *ecotypes* (forms). On average, full-grown males are slightly longer than females, and considerably heavier. Large bottlenose dolphins in the Pacific may be 3.7 m (12 ft.) and weigh 454 kg (1,000 lb.). In the Mediterranean, bottlenose dolphins can grow to 3.7 m (12 ft.) or more.

Scientists recognize two bottlenose dolphin ecotypes: coastal and offshore. In general, the coastal ecotype seems to be adapted for warm, shallow waters. Its smaller body and larger flippers suggest increased maneuverability and heat dissipation. These dolphins frequent harbors, bays, lagoons, and estuaries. The offshore ecotype seems to be adapted for cooler, deeper waters. Certain characteristics of its blood indicate that this form may be better suited for deep diving. Its larger body helps to conserve heat and defend itself against predators.

Bottlenose dolphins actively prey on a wide variety of fishes, squids, crustaceans, and shrimps. A dolphin's diet varies with its geographic location. Coastal bottlenose dolphins tend to eat fishes and bottom-dwelling invertebrates. Offshore dolphins tend to eat fishes and squid.

Bottlenose dolphins live in fluid social groups, which vary in size from about 2 to 15 individuals, although groups of more than 1,000 are sometimes spotted. Group composition and structure are typically based on age and sex. Basic social groupings tend to be nursery groups of females with calves, mixed-sex groups of juveniles, and individual or closely-bonded groups of two or three adult males.

These dolphins frequently ride the bow waves or stern wakes of boats. Both young and old dolphins chase one another, toss seaweed, carry objects around, and use objects to solicit interaction with each other. Such activity may be practice for catching food.

Bottlenose dolphins can leap as high as 4.9 m (16 ft.) out of the water.

Killer Whale
Orcinus orca

Adult male killer whales have triangular dorsal fins that may be up to 1.8m (6 ft.) tall.

The killer whale is the largest member of the dolphin family. Killer whale sizes vary between locations and populations. Adult male killer whales grow larger than adult females. Data from Icelandic killer whales indicate that an average-size male is about 5.8 to 6.7 m (19–22 ft.) long. At SeaWorld, average size for adult males is 6.6 m (21.7 ft.). Two adult male killer whales at SeaWorld weigh 4,340 kg (9,570 lb.) and 5,380 kg (11,860 lb.) Icelandic killer whale females average 4.9 to 5.8 m (16–19 ft.). At SeaWorld, average size for females is 5.5 m (18 ft.) and 2,442 kg. (5,384 lb.).

These distinctive black-and-white whales are countershaded and have disruptive coloration—a kind of camouflage in which the color pattern of an animal contradicts the animal's body shape. In the flickering, filtered sunlight of the sea, other animals may not recognize a killer whale as a potential predator.

Killer whales are found in all the oceans of the world. They're most abundant in the Arctic, the Antarctic, and areas of cold-water upwelling, where the nutrient-rich water is full of marine life to feast on. Researchers have described several ecotypes of killer whales based on the whales' size, coloration, genetics, and behavior. Three distinct ecotypes—residents, transients, and offshores—live in the eastern North Pacific, and at least three other ecotypes inhabit Antarctic waters.

Killer whales are among the most social whales. The pods consist of up to 30 individuals; a mix of males, females, and calves of varying ages. Sometimes, several smaller pods join together to form larger herds of 50 or more whales.

The worldwide population of killer whales is unknown. Although the species is not endangered, the Southern Resident killer whale population of the eastern Pacific Ocean is listed as an endangered "distinct population segment" under the Endangered Species Act of 1973.

Killer whales are the largest type of dolphin.

Baiji/ Yangtze River Dolphin
Lipotes vexillifer

The baiji has a low triangular-shaped dorsal fin and broad, rounded pectoral flippers. Photo by Stephen Leatherwood.

The baiji, a native of China's Yangtze River, hovers on the edge of extinction. Population surveys in the late 1990s estimate less than 50 or possibly even just 13 individual baijis survive, making the baiji the rarest of cetaceans.

Like other river dolphins, the baiji has a proportionally small head with a long, narrow beak, rounded melon, and tiny eyes. Unlike other river dolphins, the beak is slightly upturned. The baiji's dorsal fin is low and triangular and the pectoral flippers broad and rounded. Baiji have gray dorsal coloration that irregularly bends into white ventral coloration. Unlike most other toothed whales, female baiji grow larger than males. Male baiji grow to 2.3 m (7.5 ft.) long and weigh up to 135 kg (298 lb.) while females reach lengths of 2.6 m (8.5 ft.) and can weigh more than 240 kg (529 lb.).

Little is known about baiji behavior. Before the marked decline in numbers, baiji were usually spotted in groups of six to ten animals. From stomach content analysis, scientists have found that baiji use their numerous small, sharp teeth to feed on fishes less than 9 cm (3.5 in.) long.

Why is the baiji endangered? Baiji face a number of threats—both directly and to their environment. Many baiji are caught and killed by illegal fishing devices called rolling hooks. These long, braided lines with numerous sharp hooks are meant to catch fishes, but also accidentally ensnare baiji. Electrocution from illegal electrical fishing equipment, collisions with vessels, and injuries and death from explosions for maintaining navigation channels are also partly responsible for the decline of the baiji population.

Not only has the baiji's abundance declined, but its range has also become severely limited and its habitat degraded. Varying water levels in the Yangtze River due to dam construction and industrial development have limited available habitat to only a small portion of the main channel of the river. When the Three Gorges Dam on the upper reaches of the Yangtze is fully operational, an increase in the number of larger boats and ships utilizing improved navigation routes will increase the amount of noise pollution and the likelihood of boat-strikes to the few remaining baiji. In addition, agricultural and industrial pollution and overfishing further degrade the baiji's habitat.

Can anything be done to save the baiji? The baiji has been protected by China since 1975. In 1986, Chinese biologists began devising a protection strategy. One current proposal is to capture some of the few remaining baiji and establish a seminatural reserve site along the Yangtze River. Scientists agree that it is first necessary to find out exactly how many baiji, if any, remain before relocating any baiji. Yet, scientists debate whether or not this strategy can save the baiji from extinction.

Vaquita
Phocoena sinus

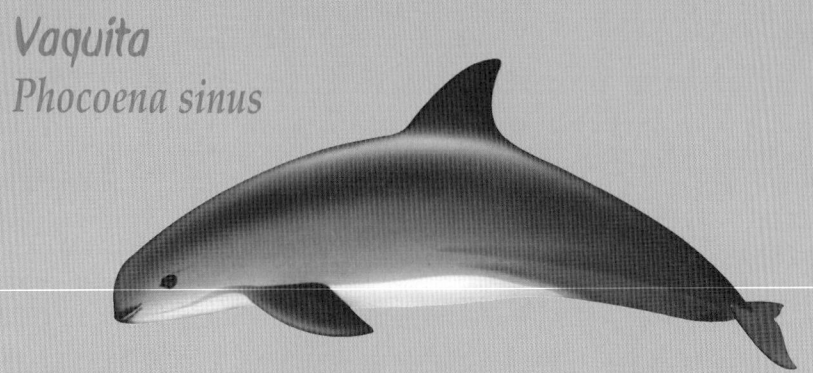

The vaquita lives only in the shallow waters of the northern Gulf of California, Mexico. Its scientific name means "porpoise of the gulf." Vaquita rarely venture beyond this small area; they have the most restricted range of any cetacean.

The vaquita is one of the smallest cetaceans. Adults range from about 1.3 to 1.5 m (4–5 ft.) in length and weigh up to 55 kg (121 lb.). Females tend to grow larger than males. A vaquita's color is a complex but subdued pattern of various shades of gray and white with darker dorsal and lighter ventral regions. Most have a bold, dark eye ring and a dark lip patch. Calves are usually darker than adults. The vaquita's dorsal fin is proportionally much taller than those of other porpoise species.

Little is known about the natural history of this seldom seen porpoise. The silty waters of its home at the mouth of the Colorado River are almost always turbid, making observation difficult. The vaquita's diet—indicated by stomach content analysis of stranded or entangled animals—consists of grunt, Gulf croakers, squids, and about 20 other species abundant in the northern Gulf of California.

The vaquita is one of the world's most endangered marine cetaceans. Scientists estimate a vaquita population size of less than 600. The vaquita's tiny, isolated population makes it highly vulnerable to human activities—especially from accidental entanglement in fishing nets set to catch other animals. Each year, at least 39 vaquita entangle and drown in *gillnets* (large flat fishing nets that entangle fish as they hang vertically in the water). This "incidental mortality" is the primary reason for the vaquita's endangered status. Gulf of California fisheries include shrimp trawling and gillnet fisheries for sharks and other fishes. The vaquita population decline was initially related to one gillnet fishery in particular: totoaba (*Totoaba macdonaldi*, a type of fish resembling the white seabass). Like the vaquita, the totoaba lives only in the upper Gulf. Vaquita are easily entangled in the larger holes of the totoaba nets. Totoaba is itself an endangered species. For many years, totoaba fishing continued with no controls until Mexico banned totoaba fishing in 1975 and the U.S. banned imports of totoaba in 1977. However, fishermen still intentionally catch totoaba, posing a continuing threat to vaquita populations.

The vaquita is protected by both United States and Mexico laws. It was placed on Mexico's endangered species list in 1978. The U.S. listed the vaquita as endangered on the ESA in 1985. The vaquita is also listed by the IUCN as critically endangered and in Appendix I of CITES. In 1993, a vaquita and totoaba biosphere reserve was established in the northern Gulf of California and, in 1997, the Committee for the Recovery of the Vaquita (CIRVA) was created. Even with international, national, and local protection and recovery efforts, incidental catch of vaquita in fishing nets continues to threaten the recovery of this species.

The vaquita's distribution is limited to the northern Gulf of California.

Life and Death in the Sea

"Whales in mid-ocean,
suspended in the waves
of the sea
great heaven of whales
in the waters,
old hierarchies.

And enormous mother
whales lie dreaming
suckling their whale-
tender young
and dreaming with
strange whale eyes
wide open in the waters
of the beginning and
the end."

*from "Whales Weep Not!"
by D.H. Lawrence*

The gestation period for bottlenose dolphins averages 12 months.

A Time to Be Born

Sexual maturity.

Sexual maturity has only been determined for a few whale species. Sexual maturity is often attained at a particular body size and is often reported as length, rather than age. It has been documented for toothed whale species that have reproduced in zoological parks. At SeaWorld Adventure Parks, animal care specialists have recorded that most bottlenose dolphin females reach sexual maturity at about 2.3 m (7.5 ft.)—sometime between the ages of five and ten years. Male bottlenose dolphins are mature at about 2.4 to 2.6 m (8–8.5 ft.), which is about eight to twelve years. Female killer whales become sexually mature when they reach about 4.6 to 4.9 m (15–16 ft.), at about 6 to 10 years, while males become sexually mature when they reach about 5.5 to 6.1 m (18–20 ft.), at about 10 to 13 years. Female sperm whales are mature at about 7 to 13 years, when they are about 8.3 to 9.2 m (27–30 ft.) long. Males don't reach maturity until ages 18 to 21, when they are about 11 to 12 m (36–39 ft.) long. Estimates of sexual maturity in baleen whales range from three to ten years depending on the species.

Gestation.

As with many factors of whale biology, gestation length has been estimated largely from wild observations. Gestation periods for baleen whales range from 10 to 14 months, depending on the species, and are linked to the annual migration cycle. Gestation estimates in toothed whales range from seven months in small toothed whales such as the Dall's porpoise to 14 to 15 months in larger toothed whales such as the sperm whale. Scientists have obtained much more accurate gestation lengths for toothed whale species that have reproduced in zoological parks. Gestation lasts about 11 to 12 months for Commerson's dolphins, 12 months for bottlenose dolphins, 14 to 15 months for beluga whales, and 17 (range 15.7 to 18) months for killer whales.

Birth.

Most baleen whale species exhibit a seasonal breeding cycle. Calves are most often born during the winter and spring in tropical and subtropical breeding grounds. The warmer climate is optimal for a calf's survival; the calf expends less energy maintaining body heat, and more energy is stored in its developing blubber layer.

For most toothed whales, particularly those that inhabit tropical to temperate waters, young can potentially be born throughout the year. Some polar toothed whales experience distinct birth seasons. Beluga whales are born from March to September, with most births occurring from May to July. All whales usually give birth to one calf at a time—twins are extremely rare. Though many whale calves are born head-first, the majority of whale births observed have been tail-first. The umbilical cord, present in all mammalian species, snaps at birth.

Commerson's calves are black and gray, attaining the more contrasting black and white pattern in about four to five months.

The calf.

A whale calf is well developed at birth. Because it is born under water, it must immediately be able to swim and follow its mother. Once out of the womb, a calf must swim to the water's surface for its first breath in the initial moments of its life.

The size of a calf depends on the species, but there isn't always a direct correlation. In general, baleen and large toothed whale calves tend to be about one-fourth the length of their mothers. Newborn baleen whale calves range from about 1.5 m (5 ft.) for pygmy right whales to about 7 m (23 ft.) for blue whales. The size of a newborn toothed whale depends on the species. At birth, Commerson's dolphin calves measure about 55 to 75 cm (22–30 in.)—as much as half the length of their mothers. Newborn sperm whales are about 4 m (13 ft.) long. Calves of other toothed whale species probably fall within this size range.

Most whale calves are born with the same coloration as adults, but some species have color variations at birth. Beluga whale calves are born gray and gradually lighten, achieving the characteristic white adult coloration near puberty. Beaked whales and pilot whales are lighter at birth and darken as adults. In killer whale calves, the white areas in adults start out as cream-colored or pale yellow. Newborn and adult color patterns also vary in some cetacean species. Commerson's calves are black and gray, attaining the more contrasting black and white pattern in about four to five months. Newborn spotted dolphins are unspotted—the spots begin to appear and spread over the body as the animals mature.

Like all mammals, whale calves are nourished by their mothers' rich milk. Calves nurse under water from nipples concealed in the mother's abdominal mammary slits. Whale milk is extremely rich in fat and protein. In baleen whales the fat content may be higher than 30%. This provides the calf with the energy to rapidly develop a thick, insulating layer of blubber. Blue whale calves gain about 90 kg (200 lb.) a day while nursing, and gray whale calves double their weight in about three months. Baleen whale calves nurse for four to eleven months, and many toothed whales may nurse for a year or more.

Milk Composition Comparisons

	Fat	Protein	Carbohydrates
blue whale	42%	12%	0.01%
fin whale	29%	11%	0.05%
humpback whale	33%	12.5%	1.1%
sperm whale	36%	4%	—
bottlenose dolphin	17%	10%	1.1%
killer whale	38%	12%	1.5%
pilot whale	44%	—	—
beluga whale	27%	11%	0.7%
harbor porpoise	46%	11%	1.3%
cow	4.0%	3.2%	4.6%
human	4.1%	1%	7%
vanilla ice cream	10%	—	—

Maternal care.

Mother-calf bonds are very strong. A mother whale stays close to her calf and attentively directs its movements. The baby swims alongside its mother's flanks and is carried in her *slip stream*—a type of hydrodynamic wake that develops as the mother swims. In baleen whales, the pair stays in close physical contact throughout the nursing period. For many toothed whale species, calves may stay with their mothers long after they are weaned, and some—like resident types of killer whales—maintain a close association with their mothers indefinitely.

Mothers are fiercely protective of their calves. In whaling years, whale hunters observed that mother whales became fiercely aggressive when they were defending their calves from attack. Growing whales seem to learn many behaviors by observing and mimicking their mothers and other older whales. Observations of whales in zoological parks suggest that females learn mothering skills from other mother whales.

Many toothed whale calves nurse for a year or more.

Gray whale calves are usually born in or near the calm, shallow-water lagoons of Baja California, Mexico. Photo by Patricia Schick.

Longevity and Mortality

For baleen whales and most toothed whales, longevity is largely unknown. In general, the larger the whale, the longer the lifespan. As with other aspects of whale biology, longevity is difficult to determine in wild populations. One method of determining age in toothed whales is examination of growth layers in the teeth. As a toothed whale ages, it periodically produces growth layer groups of dental material. Age can be estimated by examining a sliced section of a tooth and counting these layers. These estimations can be accurate in young whales, before the tooth's pulp cavity fills in, but in general are not reliable for animals older than about 20 years. To obtain a more accurate estimate of whale longevity, scientists would have the difficult task of following many, many whales throughout their lives, and this has yet to be done.

For some species of toothed whales, average longevity has been estimated. This maximum estimate ranges from about 20 years for harbor porpoises to 70 years for sperm whales. For some well-studied species, more accurate estimates have been obtained.

Most common bottlenose dolphins probably live an average of 20 years or less, though some individuals have been known to live into their 40s and 50s. At SeaWorld, several bottlenose dolphins are in their mid-thirties and some have lived into their forties. However, life span estimates can vary not just for species, but also for populations.

Because baleen whales are hard to follow over time and don't have teeth, age estimation is difficult and other methods must be used. Researchers often analyze their baleen plates and waxy ear plugs, which show some degree of regular growth rates. Scientists lack data to determine lifespan for most baleen whales, although one long term photo identification study indicates blue whales live an average of at least 31 years. Maximum lifespan estimates for baleen whales include 80 to 90 years for blue whales and fin whales, 90 to 100 years for right whales, and 60 years for minke whales.

Populations.

Accurate assessments of whale populations are nearly impossible to obtain. Whales are difficult to observe and count because they are usually seen only when they are on the surface. Population biologists must rely on complex methods of observation and statistical analysis for estimating whale numbers. One thing we know for sure is that the populations of the different whale species vary greatly.

As a management tool, scientists categorize populations of a whale species as *stocks*—geographically isolated and genetically distinct populations of a species. A species is often represented by several stocks. Some stocks of a species may be depleted, while worldwide population numbers remain high. More than 900,000 minke whales are found worldwide, yet scientists consider the West Greenland stock, which numbers about 25,000 whales, depleted. About 95% of the total population of bowhead whales currently survives in only one of four stocks while the other three face extinction. Yet, due to international protection from commercial whaling, certain stocks are recovering. One such success story features the eastern North Pacific stock of gray whale—twice hunted to the brink of extinction during peak whaling years. Following legal protection from commercial whaling in 1946, this stock of gray whales has made an astonishing comeback and numbered about 26,000 by 1998; an estimate scientists believe matches the pre-whaling population.

Scientists classify different stocks of whale species based on genetic and geographical differences. Pictured is a fin whale. Photo by Patricia Schick.

Photo-identification of individual whales, like humpback or killer whales, allows researchers to monitor the size of certain populations. Scars and other natural markings on the flukes, dorsal fins, and flanks of individual whales are photographed and catalogued. When these identified whales are resighted during subsequent years, researchers can gather information on reproductive and growth rates, differences between males and females, and migration.

Predators.

The major predator of whales is one of their own kind—killer whales. Transient killer whales hunt a variety of other dolphins and porpoises. Working together, a group of transient killer whales may even attack and kill a sperm or baleen whale substantially larger than themselves. In 1978, Hubbs-SeaWorld Research Institute scientists observed about a dozen killer whales attacking a blue whale. Swimming alongside the blue, they lunged at the much larger animal from several angles, ripping at its flesh. Scientists estimate that in Antarctic waters, minke whales make up 85% of killer whales' diets. Tooth scars on the flippers and flukes of other species are evidence of unsuccessful killer whale attacks. To a much lesser extent, pilot whales and false and pygmy killer whales sometimes prey on smaller cetacean species.

Blue whales sometimes fall prey to killer whales, which surround the much larger animal, attacking it from several angles. Photo courtesy of Hubbs-SeaWorld Research Institute.

Large sharks occasionally prey on some whales, particularly those that are ill, injured, or very young. Large predatory sharks, such as great white, tiger, bull, and dusky sharks, sometimes prey on the smaller species of toothed whales. One study found that about 74% of bottlenose dolphins in Shark Bay, Western Australia have scars from shark bites—mostly from tiger sharks. Large sharks will also scavenge from large whale carcasses although evidence of direct shark attacks on baleen whales is scarce.

Although polar bears mainly hunt seals, they also actively prey on belugas and narwhals. In some areas, polar bears fish for these whales at breathing holes in the ice, swiping the whales out of the water when they come up for a breath of air. Polar bears also opportunistically prey on belugas that are temporarily beached by outgoing tides and even attack belugas swimming near the edges of the ice or shore.

Disease and parasitism.

As in any animal population, a variety of diseases can be responsible for whale mortality. Whales may develop stomach ulcers, skin diseases, tumors, heart disease, urogenital disorders, and respiratory disorders. They also suffer from viral, bacterial, and fungal infections.

All whales are susceptible to a variety of parasites. Internal parasites include tapeworms, roundworms, and flukes. These

SeaWorld animal care specialists rescue a bottlenose dolphin with a shark bite wound.

parasites can infest and cause damage to the organs and each parasite specializes in a specific part of the body. In most cases, parasite infestations alone are unlikely to debilitate otherwise healthy animals, but they may harm animals that are already weakened by other illnesses or injuries.

The most common external parasites of whales are barnacles and whale lice. These are especially prevalent on the slower moving baleen whales. Barnacles cement onto the skin around a whale's head, throat grooves, blowhole, and genital region, and feed on plankton as the whale swims. Gray whales are heavily infested with host-specific species of barnacles. Humpbacks also can carry a heavy barnacle load—one male humpback had 450 kg (992 lb.) of barnacles attached to its skin. Mature male beaked and bottlenose whales often have stalked barnacles attached to their erupted teeth.

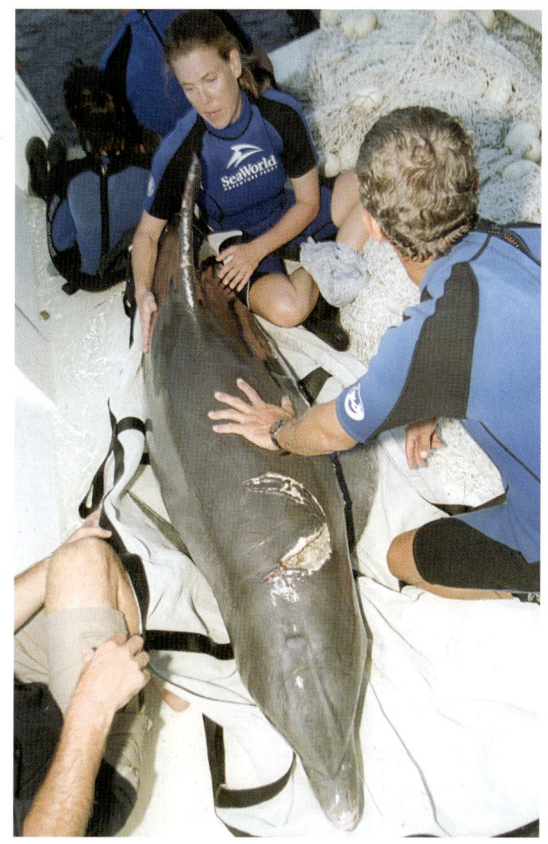

Gray whales are often encrusted with certain species of whale lice and barnacles.

Whale lice also attach to the skin of many whales. Whale lice are not true lice but, instead, are a type of amphipod crustacean that feeds on dead skin and damaged tissue. Although external parasites can add to a whale's weight load they usually don't affect the overall health of their host.

Strandings.

A stranded animal is a live marine animal that is out of its element, such as a whale that ends up on the beach. In general, a whale strands if it has a serious debilitating illness or injury, or if it is too weak to hunt or swim.

Why do whales strand? Some whales that strand may be ill or injured, while others seem healthy. Some scientists have theorized

All toothed whale species are known to strand. Pilot whales are often associated with mass strandings.

that healthy whales may strand when they make mistakes related to their ability to follow geomagnetic contours of the earth. Whales may rely on geomagnetic cues to provide information about their relative position. Another theory is that toothed whales may strand if their echolocation ability becomes impaired.

All species of toothed whales are known to strand. Individuals of coastal species are more commonly found stranded than oceanic species. Most toothed whales that live in groups tend to strand in groups. False killer whales and pilot whales—both highly social oceanic toothed whales—are notorious for mass strandings. SeaWorld Orlando has participated in rescue efforts for mass-stranded pilot whales and false killer whales. While none of the stranded animals survived, animal care experts were able to collect valuable data that may help scientists to better understand why whales strand. Whales that inhabit polar regions may become entrapped in ice during the fall when the ice pack advances. These animals are also considered stranded.

Since the late 1960s, mass strandings of beaked whales, and other deep diving whales, have been correlated with the use of high-intensity sonar. A direct causal link has yet to be demonstrated. The available reports of an increase in beaked whale strandings are difficult to evaluate because stranding data on these species are notoriously sparse and records collected at strandings weren't always adequate. Over the last half of the 20th century, the U.S. and other countries established formal stranding networks; improving data collection procedures greatly. It is possible that some of the apparent recent increase in beaked whale strandings is just the result of more search effort and better record keeping. Speculations in popular news stories should be interpreted with care—many strandings of a wide range of cetacean species are now being attributed to sonars without good evidence.

Human impact.

Indigenous and small-scale whaling. Indigenous people from coastal areas throughout the world have relied on various whale species for subsistence for thousands of years and continue to do so in many parts of the world today. Natives of coastal arctic villages hunt small numbers of bowhead, minke, and gray whales. People of Greenland, Siberia, and the United States hunt narwhals and belugas; and villagers in Indonesia hunt sperm whales, killer

Large-scale commercial whaling has been devastating to all baleen whale species, and has impacted several toothed whale species.
Photo by Hubbs-SeaWorld Research Institute.

whales, pilot whales, and several species of dolphins. People in several other small countries also hunt small numbers of toothed whales including Cuvier's and Baird's beaked whales, northern bottlenose whales, killer whales, false killer whales, melon-headed whales, pygmy killer whales, pilot whales, Atlantic white-sided dolphins, harbor porpoises, and Dall's porpoises.

Large-scale and commercial hunting. Historically, native subsistence hunting has not had a significant impact on whale populations—only small numbers are taken. But when whale hunting went from small-scale to large-scale, many populations sustained crippling blows from which most have not recovered. Whale oil was used for lighting, heating, and lubrication; as a base for the manufacture of soaps and paints; and in the processing of textiles and rope. Baleen was used to make corset stays, umbrella ribs, fishing rods, buggy whips, carriage springs, skirt hoops, brushes, and nets.

The commercial whaling industry began to expand in the 12th century. Whalers targeted the massive baleen whales, especially the right whales, so named because whalers considered them the "right" whales to hunt because they have immense amounts of blubber and baleen, they are a coastal species, they are slow swimmers, and their bodies float when dead, making them easier to recover. As right whales became rare, the whaling industry sought out other species to harvest. Then in the 19th century, with improved hunting weapons and boats, faster species such as humpback, blue, and fin whales were killed in large numbers. Minke whales became a major target in the 1930s, when they were hunted because larger species were depleted.

Although most people associate whaling with the baleen whales, whalers also hunted various species of toothed whales—especially sperm whales. As commercial whaling depleted the right whales by the early 18th century, more and more commercial fisheries around the world focused on sperm whales. The sperm whale industry centered around the high quality of candle wax and lamp oil produced from the whale's spermaceti and oil from the adjacent junk—both in the head region of the whale. Although rarely found in the intestines of some sperm whales, ambergris was also prized as a perfume fixative.

Markets for whale products expanded to the 20th century, and more modern harpoons, explosives, and factory-type processing ships were used to hunt and harvest baleen whales and sperm whales. Fortunately, petroleum, cottonseed oil, linseed oil, and palmseed oil have replaced whale oil products. In some countries there is still a market for certain types of whale meat, which is considered a delicacy.

Entanglement in fishing gear. In more recent years, whale populations have suffered significant impact due to accidental entanglement in fishing nets and gear set for fishes and other marine animals. Whales that are injured or killed and discarded in the course of fishing operations are called *bycatch*. Experts have concluded that it's likely hundreds of thousands of marine mammals are killed as bycatch each year. The incidental capture of whales, particularly toothed whales, in the course of fishing operations occurs throughout the world, in virtually all habitats. For some endangered species such as the vaquita, bycatch remains the primary threat to their survival.

The purse seine fishery in the Eastern Tropical Pacific (ETP) Ocean has long been a concern for dolphin conservation. Tuna and certain kinds of dolphins (particularly spinner dolphins, spotted dolphins,

Many toothed whales, including vaquitas, accidentally entangle in fishing nets set for fishes and other aquatic animals. Photo by Flip Nicklin, (Minden Pictures).

short-beaked common dolphins, and striped dolphins) are often found together. Locating groups of these dolphins on the ocean surface can be a reliable way to find tuna that are below the surface. It used to be common practice for purse seiners fishing for tuna to set their nets around groups of these dolphins. When the net was hauled in, it sometimes entangled dolphins. Since the fishery began in the late 1950s, experts estimate that as many as 6 million dolphins have been killed as bycatch.

Net modifications and release programs dramatically reduced dolphin mortality. In 1990 the United States passed the Dolphin Protection Consumer Information Act (DPCIA). The DPCIA created a "dolphin-safe" certification for tuna caught by methods that don't involve dolphin bycatch. In response, the U.S. tuna industry developed a tracking system and decreased the number of times they set nets around dolphins. In 1999, the major fishing countries in the ETP signed the binding Agreement on the International Dolphin Conservation Program (AIDCP) to reduce dolphin bycatch in the tuna purse-seine fishery. The Agreement sets annual limits and recommends that fishers seek alternative means of catching tunas not in association with dolphins. Fishermen have dramatically reduced dolphin bycatch in the ETP to about 3,000 animals per year.

Pollution. Chemicals that are used on land enter waterways through runoff and eventually end up in the oceans as pollution. Industrial pollutants are introduced to the marine environment through mining operations, agriculture, pulp mills, and other coastal industrial development. Household and garden pesticides can enter waterways through sewers and storm drains.

Persistent organic pollutants (POPs) are pollutants that don't break down in the marine environment. These types of pollutants can enter the ocean food chain and become concentrated in the bodies of whales and other marine predators. Some of these pollutants (which may not be harmful in small quantities) are stored in an animal's body tissues after they are ingested. These fat-soluble molecules accumulate in fats, such as blubber. When ingested, POPs aren't metabolized or eliminated. Prey animals that contain such toxins in their bodies pass the toxins on to animals higher in the food chain. Pollutants can become concentrated and reach dangerous levels in the bodies of large predators. Many studies have documented high levels of POPs in belugas in the St. Lawrence River Estuary. Similar studies have found that killer whales in the eastern North Pacific Ocean are also heavily contaminated.

Habitat destruction. Not just a threat to tropical rainforests, habitat destruction also threatens populations of coastal and freshwater whales. When dams are built or shorelines are altered along river systems, water level changes can result in reduced habitat and isolated populations for river dolphins. The baiji is one notable species that has suffered, due in large part to water construction projects. Dams and levees prevent the dolphins and their food fish from traveling to traditional feeding and breeding areas. Combined with pollution, overfishing, and bycatch, this habitat destruction has made the baiji one of the world's most endangered animals.

With fewer than 50 individuals remaining, the baiji—or Yangtze River dolphin—is the most endangered cetacean species. Photo by Stephen Leatherwood.

Competition with commercial fisheries. In many areas throughout the world, toothed whales and fishermen compete for the same fish. Prey populations in many areas become overfished, leading to depleted populations of toothed whales. In the Mediterranean and Black Seas, for example, prey depletion by commercial fisheries caused significant drops in populations of bottlenose dolphins, short-beaked common dolphins, striped dolphins, and harbor porpoises. Some toothed whales occasionally "steal" fish from fishing nets or longlines. Such interactions not only lead to product loss for fishermen, but often damage or destroy fishing gear. When catches decline, fishermen sometimes believe that local populations of toothed whales are the cause. In some areas, fishermen organize whale or dolphin kills in an effort to control their populations.

Saving the Whales

Many baleen whale stocks, severely depleted due to commercial whaling, are still endangered or threatened. More recently, several toothed whale stocks have also become endangered due to entanglement, habitat loss, and other threats.

Legal Protection of Whales.

The International Whaling Commission (IWC). In 1946, 14 countries signed the International Whaling Convention for the regulation of whaling, thus forming the International Whaling Commission (IWC). The purpose of the IWC is to manage whale stocks and protect their futures. Currently, the IWC monitors whale populations through scientific advisory groups and makes management proposals to member nations. For instance, the IWC makes recommendations on how many whales natives of traditional whaling countries should harvest in subsistence hunting.

In 1986, the IWC declared a moratorium on commercial whaling. However, the moratorium does allow certain provisions for scientific research and native subsistence hunting. At times various nations threaten to ignore the IWC recommendations and resume commercial whaling. If this were to happen, the IWC would have no means by which to enforce its regulations.

Currently the IWC has no jurisdiction over small cetaceans. However, now that the harvest of most baleen whales and sperm

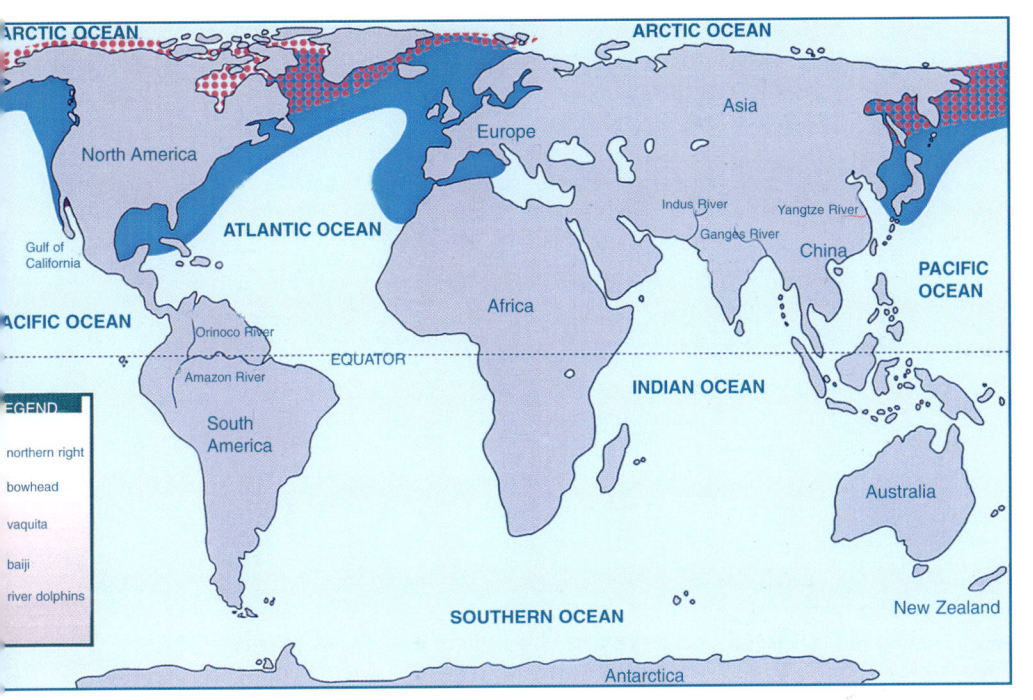

Distribution of the world's most endangered whales.

whales has stopped, the IWC has expressed interest in playing a role in managing small cetacean populations as well.

The U.S. Marine Mammal Protection Act of 1972 (MMPA). The MMPA, reauthorized in 2006, makes it illegal to hunt or harass any marine mammal in U.S waters. According to the MMPA, all whales in U.S. waters (baleen and toothed) are under the jurisdiction of the National Oceanic and Atmospheric Administration (NOAA). The primary objective of the MMPA is to maintain the health and stability of the marine ecosystem and to obtain and maintain an optimum sustainable population of marine mammals. The MMPA, like the IWC, does allow certain provisions for native subsistence hunting; a restricted amount of incidental take; and research, education, and public display.

The Endangered Species Act (ESA). Seven species of baleen whales and four species of toothed whales are listed as "endangered" under the Endangered Species Act of 1973. A species is considered endangered if it is in danger of extinction.

The eastern North Pacific stock of California gray whale, twice hunted to the brink of extinction, was listed among the endangered whales. But legally protected since 1946, the stock has made a

The IUCN/World Conservation Union lists beluga whales as vulnerable to extinction in the wild.

strong recovery. In 1998, the population numbered about 26,000; a figure that scientists believe matches the pre-whaling numbers. In 1994, the eastern North Pacific stock of gray whales was removed from the Endangered Species List. However, the western North Pacific stock, which only numbers about 100 whales, remains endangered.

In 2005, the ESA designated the Southern Resident population of killer whales as an endangered Discreet Population Segment (DPS). This population declined 20% in the 1990s and currently stands at about 89 whales. This DPS faces risks including vessel traffic, toxic chemicals and competition for food, especially salmon. The small DPS is susceptible to potential catastrophic risks, such as disease or oil spills.

IUCN/The World Conservation Union. IUCN/The World Conservation Union (International Union for Conservation of Nature and Natural Resources) is a worldwide conservation organization. Established in 1948, it links government agencies, non-government agencies, and independent states to encourage a worldwide approach to conservation. The *IUCN Red List* is a system for assessing an animal's relative risk of extinction. Its goal is to categorize and raise global awareness of species that face a high risk of extinction. The IUCN's Species Survival Commission (SSC) works with zoological parks and aquariums to maintain worldwide biological diversity. Its Cetacean Specialist Group is comprised of many whale experts that coordinate programs to conserve threatened whale species.

The IUCN classifies the baiji and the vaquita as "Critically Endangered." Species in this category face an extremely high risk of extinction in the immediate future. The Sei whale, blue whale, fin whale, northern right whale, Indus and Ganges river dolphins, and Hector's dolphin are all red-listed as "Endangered"—indicating a very high risk of extinction in the near future. The humpback whale, sperm whale, boto, beluga whale, and harbor porpoise are classified as "Vulnerable." These whales face a high risk of extinction in the medium-term future. Species classified as "Lower Risk/conservation dependent" are not endangered, but may be

Endangered Whales

whale	ESA	IUCN
bowhead	E	
Sei	E	E
blue	E	E
fin	E	E
gray	E (western Pacific pop. only)	
humpback	E	V
northern right	E	E
southern right	E	
sperm	E	V
baiji	E	Cr
Indus & Ganges river dolphin	E	E
Amazon river dolphin		V
killer whale	E (Southern Resident pop. only)	
beluga		V
vaquita	E	Cr
harbor porpoise		V
Hector's dolphin		E

Status listings: Vulnerable (V), Endangered (E), Critically Endangered (Cr).

endangered within five years unless current conservation programs continue. This category includes a number of whale species. Many whales that do not qualify for Conservation Dependent are listed as "Lower Risk/least concern." Many other cetaceans fall into a category called "Data Deficient." After evaluating these species, the IUCN has determined that there is not enough information to assess the risk of extinction.

The Convention on International Trade in Endangered Species of Wild Fauna and Flora (CITES). CITES is an international treaty developed in 1973 to regulate trade in certain wildlife species. CITES protects all whales. All species of baleen whales and 13 species of toothed whales are listed under CITES Appendix I—the most endangered of CITES-listed animals and plants. CITES prohibits commercial international trade in specimens of Appendix I species. CITES lists all other toothed whales in Appendix II as species not currently considered threatened with extinction, but that may become so unless trade is closely controlled.

Marine zoological parks.

Marine zoological parks provide opportunities for scientists and the public to learn, up-close, about whales and how human activities may impact their survival. In the protected environment of a zoological park, scientists can examine aspects of whale biology that are difficult to study in the wild. Taking routine measurements of the many killer whale calves born and raised at SeaWorld parks has enabled researchers to assess accurate growth curves, something that was almost impossible to obtain through observations of wild killer whale groups. In addition, SeaWorld researchers have successfully bred several species of whales through artificial insemination, which could become a valuable tool in future breeding programs of rarer species of whales.

Rescue, rehabilitation, and release. Marine life parks that rescue, rehabilitate and release stranded, injured, ill, or orphaned whales add to the body of research on whales. SeaWorld parks have rescued many species of whales and dolphins, including gray whales, a Bryde's whale, minke whales, sperm whales, both pygmy and dwarf sperm whales, common dolphins, bottlenose dolphins, Risso's dolphins, Pacific white-sided dolphins, spotted dolphins, spinner dolphins, northern right whale dolphins, killer whales, and both false and pygmy killer whales.

In 1997, SeaWorld became involved in one of its most acclaimed rehabilitation projects to date—raising a baby gray whale. The gray whale calf, named J.J., stranded in the surf at Marina del Rey, California. She was barely clinging to life when she was brought to SeaWorld. The calf made a remarkable recovery, and after 15 months of expert care, J.J. was returned home to the sea. Insight gained from caring for rescued whales and dolphins adds to the growing body of knowledge that helps us to care for cetaceans and to better understand cetacean biology.

SeaWorld animal care specialists help care for a rescued pygmy sperm whale (top) and northern right whale dolphin (bottom).

Zoological parks have made great strides in the whale conservation effort. Researchers hope that information gained by rehabilitating stranded whales, like J.J. the gray whale, will be useful in the battle to save species that face extinction.

A Splash of Education. The unique opportunity to observe and learn directly from live animals at zoological parks, such as SeaWorld, increases public awareness and appreciation of wildlife. Most people do not have the opportunity to observe whales in the wild. At SeaWorld parks, people experience marine wildlife in a personal way that isn't possible through books, television, films, or the Internet. In 2005, a Harris Interactive® poll showed that most adults in the United States agree that visiting zoological parks and aquariums encourages conservation efforts for animals. In addition, 95% of the respondents believed that seeing animals up-close at aquariums and zoological parks cultivates a greater appreciation for animals and conservation in children.

SeaWorld & Busch Gardens Conservation Fund.

Established in 2003, the non-profit SeaWorld & Busch Gardens Conservation Fund works on behalf of wildlife and habitats worldwide. The goal of the Fund is to encourage sustainable solutions by supporting critical conservation initiatives worldwide. The Fund conducts grant awards each year. Selected projects are science-based, solution-driven and community-oriented—attributes needed to achieve effective and long-term conservation success. The Fund accepts donations to support conservation projects in the U.S. and around the world with 100% of donations going directly to selected projects. In addition to other marine and terrestrial projects, the Fund supports many different programs related to whale conservation.

One study sponsored by the Fund is the U.K.'s Royal Society for Nature Conservation/The Wildlife Trust development and testing of a modified pinger to address the problem of harbor porpoises habituating to pingers on fishing nets or being frightened away from important foraging areas.

Another Fund grant helped fund a Texas A&M study of the ecology and population biology of the dolphins in a newly designated marine reserve in the Pemba Island region of Zanzibar Archipelago (Tanzania). The study assessed potential environmental implications of dolphin-watch ecotourism, set out appropriate mitigation measures, and established a scientific basis for a long-term management plan.

Researchers from Hawaii Pacific University used a SeaWorld & Busch Gardens Conservation Fund grant to fund the attachment of satellite transmitters and time depth recorders to rough-toothed dolphins and melon-headed whales in French Polynesia. This study helped establish dive profiles and movement patterns for these species. Basic information on habitat use is required to investigate potential causes of stranding events. Marine mammal biology students at the university share findings in an engaging, kid-friendly way with local school children to promote marine conservation throughout Hawaii and French Polynesia.

The Fund provided a grant to the Wildlife in Need Foundation of Lompoc, California to supports the rescue, rehabilitation and release of stranded whales, including bottlenose dolphins, in the Phillipines.

In November 2006, the SeaWorld & Busch Gardens Conservation Fund, along with Anheuser-Busch and the Hubbs-SeaWorld Research Institute, supported the Yangtze Freshwater Dolphin Expedition to document the populations of the critically endangered baiji and the endangered Yangtze finless porpoise. Scientists from six different nations conducted the census, documented population locations, and conducted water quality tests to determine habitat quality. Data gathered during the intensive, six-week field survey will be published and disseminated to Chinese authorities and research institutes as the foundation for a long-term conservation strategy.

Hubbs-SeaWorld Research Institute.

Even before the creation of the SeaWorld & Busch Gardens Conservation Fund, SeaWorld supported conservation research on whales. Since 1965, SeaWorld parks and the Hubbs-SeaWorld Research Institute have collaborated with state and federal agencies in the rescue and rehabilitation of stranded cetaceans, and the parks have handled more than 350 such rescues. When possible, the animals are returned to sea, often with radio or satellite transmitters attached.

The database for the Southeastern United States Marine Mammal Stranding Network is housed at SeaWorld Orlando and maintained by SeaWorld and H-SWRI staff. SeaWorld and H-SWRI conduct studies on both living and dead stranded cetaceans. Studies include feeding ecology, parasitology, age estimation, mortality rates, tracking of released animals and various aspects of cetacean life history.

H-SWRI scientists are also studying the development of vocal dialects in killer whale calves born at SeaWorld to understand how group-specific vocalizations relate to animal communication and behavior. Because killer whale vocal development bears striking similarities to our own, the research provides insight into the biological basis of human language. The knowledge gained from this research may also help marine scientists better understand and protect killer whales in the wild.

SeaWorld has also supported the Hubbs-SeaWorld Research Institute's "novel objects" study. This study applies bio-acoustics expertise and scientific innovation to find ways to keep marine mammals from becoming entangled in fishing gear.

The satellite transmitter attached to the dorsal fin of this common dolphin allowed researchers from H-SWRI to track the movement patterns of this animal after its release.

SeaWorld parks provide opportunities for safe and exhilarating interaction with a variety of whales.

Wild encounters with whales.

For those who do get the opportunity to see whales in the wild, whale watching is an unforgettable experience. It's a great thrill to encounter whales and dolphins in the wild, and a great temptation to touch or feed them. But marine mammals are protected by laws. According to the Marine Mammal Protection Act, it is illegal even to approach marine mammals in the wild in United States waters. NOAA has developed "Marine wildlife viewing guidelines" to protect marine animals. Among other recommendations, the guidelines instruct whale watchers to keep their distance. Chasing or harassing animals, impeding their right of way, and touching and feeding animals are not allowed. This is for both protection of the whales and of people. Often, wild animals are fed inappropriate food items that can make the animal very ill. If these animals become accustomed to being approached and fed by humans, they may not be willing to hunt and feed on their own. Sometimes, these animals become a nuisance, prompting humans to control them by removing or even killing them.

Human interaction may also disrupt and endanger normal animal behaviors such as reproduction and care of their young. And cetaceans are very large, powerful animals.

Dolphins may appear playful, but are capable of injuring people. Leaving nature alone is perhaps the single most significant thing people can do to help preserve it.

So what do we know about whales? Most people now realize that whales are mammals, not fish, with complex behaviors and unique adaptations to their watery world. Sophisticated scientific advances in research and decades of close observation have provided us with some information on cetacean distributions, physiology, vocalizations, behavior, and natural history, yet much remains a mystery. In the words of the 19th century whaler turned naturalist, Charles Scammon, "…many of the characteristic actions of whales are so secretly performed that years of ordinary observation may be insufficient for their discovery." What was true for the mid 19th century is true today—and these powerful creatures continue to fascinate and enthrall us.

Even though scientists have learned much through decades of research on whales, these magnificent marine mammals continue to capture our fascination. Pictured are killer whales.

Appendix: Whale Classification

SUBORDER MYSTICETI: THE BALEEN WHALES

Family Balaenidae: the right whales
bowhead whale, *Balaena mysticetus*
northern right whale, *Eubalaena glacialis*
southern right whale, *Eubalaena australis*

Family Neobalaenidae
pygmy right whale, *Caperea marginata*

Family Balaenopteridae: the rorqual whales
common minke whale, *Balaenoptera acutorostrata*
Antarctic minke whale, *Balaenoptera bonarensis*
Sei whale, *Balaenoptera borealis*
Bryde's whale, *Balaenoptera edeni*
blue whale, *Balaenoptera musculus*
Omura's whale, *Balaenoptera omurai*
fin whale, *Balaenoptera physalus*
humpback whale, *Megaptera novaeangliae*

Family Eschrichtiidae
gray whale, *Eschrichtius robustus*

SUBORDER ODONTOCETI: THE TOOTHED WHALES

Family Delphinidae (oceanic dolphins)
Atlantic humpbacked dolphin, *Sousa teuszii*
Atlantic spotted dolphin, *Stenella frontalis*
Atlantic white-sided dolphin, *Lagenorhynchus acutus*
Australian snubfin dolphin, *Orcaella heinsohni*
black dolphin, *Cephalorhynchus eutropia*
bottlenose dolphin, *Tursiops truncatus*
Commerson's dolphin, *Cephalorhynchus commersonii*
dusky dolphin, *Lagenorhynchus obscurus*
false killer whale, *Pseudorca crassidens*
Fraser's dolphin, *Lagenodelphis hosei*
Heaviside's dolphin, *Cephalorhynchus heavisidii*
Hector's dolphin, *Cephalorhynchus hectori*
hourglass dolphin, *Lagenorhynchus cruciger*
Indian humpbacked dolphin, *Sousa plumbea*

Indian Ocean bottlenose dolphin, *Tursiops aduncus*
Indo-Pacific humpbacked dolphin, *Sousa chinensis*
Irrawaddy dolphin, *Orcaella brevirostris*
killer whale, *Orcinus orca*
long-beaked common dolphin, *Delphinus capensis*
long-finned pilot whale, *Globicephala melas*
long-snouted spinner dolphin, *Stenella longirostris*
melon-headed whale, *Peponocephala electra*
northern right whale dolphin, *Lissodelphis borealis*
Pacific white-sided dolphin, *Lagenorhynchus obliquidens*
Peale's dolphin, *Lagenorhynchus australis*
pygmy killer whale, *Feresa attenuata*
Risso's dolphin, *Grampus griseus*
rough-toothed dolphin, *Steno bredanensis*
short-beaked common dolphin, *Delphinus delphis*
short-finned pilot whale, *Globicephala macrorhynchus*
short-snouted spinner dolphin, *Stenella clymene*
southern right whale dolphin, *Lissodelphis peronii*
spotted dolphin, *Stenella attenuata*
striped dolphin, *Stenella coeruleoalba*
tucuxi, *Sotalia fluviatilis*
white-beaked dolphin, *Lagenorhynchus albirostris*

Family Physeteridae
sperm whale, *Physeter macrocephalus*

Family Kogiidae
dwarf sperm whale, *Kogia simus*
pygmy sperm whale, *Kogia breviceps*

Family Ziphiidae (beaked whales)
Andrews's beaked whale, *Mesoplodon bowdoini*
Arnoux's beaked whale, *Berardius arnuxii*
Baird's beaked whale, *Berardius bairdii*
Blainville's beaked whale, *Mesoplodon densirostris*
Cuvier's beaked whale, *Ziphius cavirostris*
Gervais' beaked whale, *Mesoplodon europaeus*
ginkgo-toothed beaked whale, *Mesoplodon ginkgodensis*
Gray's beaked whale, *Mesoplodon grayi*
Hector's beaked whale, *Mesoplodon hectori*
Hubbs's beaked whale, *Mesoplodon carlhubbsi*
Longman's beaked whale (also called Indo-Pacific beaked whale), *Indopacetus pacificus*

northern bottlenose whale, *Hyperoodon ampullatus*
Perrin's beaked whale, *Mesoplodon perrini*
pygmy beaked whale, *Mesoplodon peruvianus*
southern bottlenose whale, *Hyperoodon planifrons*
spade-toothed whale, *Mesoplodon traversii*
Sowerby's beaked whale, *Mesoplodon bidens*
Stejneger's beaked whale, *Mesoplodon stejnegeri*
strap-toothed whale, *Mesoplodon layardii*
Tasman beaked whale, *Tasmacetus shepardi*
True's beaked whale, *Mesoplodon mirus*

Family Platanistidae
Ganges and Indus River dolphins, *Platanista gangetica*
Ganges River dolphin (also called the susu and the Ganges susu), *P.g. gangetica*
Indus River dolphin (also called the bhulan and the Indus susu), *P.g. minor*

Family Iniidae
boto (also called the Amazon river dolphin and the pink dolphin), *Inia geoffrensis*

Family Lipotidae
baiji (also called the Yangtze River dolphin and the Chinese River dolphin), *Lipotes vexillifer*

Family Pontoporiidae
Franciscana (also called the La Plata dolphin), *Pontoporia blainvillei*

Family Monodontidae
beluga (also called the white whale), *Delphinapterus leucas*
narwhal, *Monodon monoceros*

Family Phocoenidae (porpoises)
Burmeister's porpoise, *Phocoena spinipinnis*
Dall's porpoise, *Phocoenoides dalli*
finless porpoise, *Neophocaena phocaenoides*
harbor porpoise, *Phocoena phocoena*
spectacled porpoise, *Phocoena dioptrica*
vaquita, *Phocoena sinus*

Glossary

A
amphipod—a small shrimplike crustacean in the order Amphipoda.

B
baleen—parallel plates, composed of keratin, that grow from the upper jaw of baleen whales for filtering food from the water.
barnacle—marine crustaceans in the subclass Cirripedia. Adults form a hard outer shell and attach to a solid surface. Some even remain attached to whale skin.
behavior—the way an animal acts.
bioacoustics—the study of sounds produced or received by living organisms.
blow—the visible exhalation of a whale.
blowhole—the opening to the lungs of a whale, similar to a human's nostrils.
blubber—a layer of fat cells and fibrous connective tissue, between the skin and muscle of most marine mammals.
breach—a behavior in which a whale jumps out of the water and lands on its side or back.
bull—the adult males of certain large marine mammals, including whales and manatees, walruses, seals, and sea lions.
bycatch—animals unintentionally caught during fishing operations.

C
calf—the young of whales, walruses, and manatees.
callosities—raised, roughened patches of skin on a right whale's head. Large whale lice colonies typically dwell among the callosities. A right whale's callosities are distinct enough to be useful in photo identification of individuals.
cetacean—the order of marine mammals that includes all whales, dolphins, and porpoises.
communicate—to convey information.
countershading—type of camouflage in which the coloration of the dorsal side of an animal is darker than the ventral side.

D
disruptive coloration—color patterns that obscure the outline of an animal by contradicting the animal's body shape or by drawing attention to certain highly distinctive elements of the pattern.
dorsal—the back side of an animal.
dorsal fin—the fin on the back of a whale or other aquatic animal.

E
echolocate—to locate objects by emitting sound waves and interpreting the resulting echo.
ecotype—a form of a species often with behavioral/anatomical differences from other forms.

F
falcate—refers to a dorsal fin that is sickle shaped or curved back.
flipper—a broad, flat limb supported by bones and modified for swimming.
flukes—the two horizontal lobes of a whale's tail, made of connective tissue, not bone.
fusiform—a shape that is tapered at both ends.

G
gestation—the period during which offspring are developing and carried within the mother's uterus.

H
habitat—the place where an animal lives.
hemoglobin—the oxygen-carrying molecule of a red blood cell.

K
krill—a small shrimplike crustacean in the family Euphasiidae, often found clustered in huge numbers as zooplankton.

L
lobtailing—a behavior in which a cetacean slaps the surface with it's flukes.

M
mass strand—when two or more individual whales come ashore.
melon—the rounded, fat-filled region of the head of most toothed whales.

myoglobin—an iron-containing protein in the muscle tissue. Myoglobin transports and stores oxygen.

P
pectoral flippers—the broad, flat forelimbs of a whale.
pec-slapping—a behavior in which a whale slaps one or both pectoral flippers on the surface.
plankton—tiny plants and animals that drift in oceans, lakes, ponds, and rivers.
pod—a closely-bonded, social group of whale.

R
rake—a behavior in which a toothed whale scratches another whale with its teeth.
rorqual—a family of baleen whales that includes blue, fin, humpback, minke, sei, and Bryde's whales.
rostrum—a beaklike or snoutlike projection.

S
social—animals of the same species that frequently interact in a nonaggressive way.
spyhop—a behavior in which a whale raises its head vertically out of the water enough so that it can look around above the water.

T
tail stock—the portion of a whale's body behind the dorsal fin to just in front of the flukes.
thermoregulation—processes by which an animal regulates body temperature.

V
ventral—the belly side of an animal.

W
whale—any member of the mammalian order Cetacea including whales, dolphins, and porpoises. Sometimes used to refer to just the larger cetaceans.
whale lice—amphipod crustaceans in the family Cyamidae. Many species colonize and feed on the skin of whales.

More Information

For experienced readers

Au, Whitlow W.L. *The Sonar of Dolphins*. New York: Springer-Verlag Inc., 1993.

Au, Whitlow W.L., Arthur N. Popper, and Richard R. Fay, eds. *Hearing by Whales and Dolphins*. New York: Springer-Verlag, 2000.

Berta, Annalisa, James L. Sumich, and Kit M. Kovacs. *Marine Mammals: Evolutionary Biology*, 2nd ed. Amsterdam: Academic Press, 2006.

Herman, Louis M., ed. *Cetacean Behavior: Mechanisms and Functions*. New York: John Wiley and Sons, 1980.

Nowak, Ronald, M. *Walker's Marine Mammals of the World*. Baltimore: The John Hopkins University Press. 2003.

*Nuzzolo, Deborah. *The Commerson's Dolphin Story*. San Diego: Sea World, Inc., 2004.

*Nuzzolo, Deborah. *Dolphin Discovery: Bottlenose Dolphin Training and Discovery*. San Diego: Sea World, Inc., 2003.

*Parham, Donna. *To the Rescue! The SeaWorld/Busch Gardens Animal Rescue and Rehabilitation Program*. San Diego: Sea World, Inc., 2005.

*Rake, Jody. Behind the Scenes: *Animal Training at SeaWorld, Busch Gardens, and Discovery Cove*. San Diego: Sea World, Inc., 2003.

Reeves, Randall R., Brent S. Stewart, Phillip J. Clapman, and James A. Powell. *Guide to Marine Mammals of the World*. New York: Alfred A. Knopf, 2002.

Reynolds, John E., and Sentiel A. Rommel, eds. *Biology of Marine Mammals*. Washington: Smithsonian Institution Press, 1999.

*Wlodarski, Loran. *Killer Whales: Creatures of Legend and Wonder*. Orlando: Sea World, Inc., 2000.

Wursig, Bernd and J.G.M. Thewissen, eds. *Encyclopedia of Marine Mammals*. San Diego: Academic Press, 2002.

*Available at SeaWorld. Call **(800) 25-SHAMU** and press 46 to request an Educational Resources Catalog.

For young readers

Brust, Beth Wagner. W. *Zoobooks: Dolphins and Porpoises*. Poway, CA: Wildlife Education, Ltd., 2004.

Hatherly, Janelle and Delia Nicholls. *Dolphins and Porpoises: Great Creatures of the World*. New York: Facts on File, Inc., 1990.

*Nuzzolo, Deborah. *This is a Dolphin*. San Diego: Sea World, Inc., 2002.

Parker, Steve. *Whales and Dolphins*. San Francisco: Sierra Club Books for Children, 1994.

Resnick, Jane. *All About training Shamu*. Bridgeport, CT: Third Story Books, 1994.

Rinard, Judith E. *Dolphins: Our Friends in the Sea: Dolphins and Other Toothed Whales*. Washington D.C.: The National Geographic Society, 1986.

Wexo, John Bonnett. *Zoobooks: Whales*. San Diego: Wildlife Education, Ltd.,1996.

Worth, Bonnie. *A Whale of a Tale!* New York: Random House, 2006.

Web sites

Alliance of Marine Mammal Parks and Aquariums. *ammpa.org*
Association of Zoos and Aquariums. *aza.org*
CITES. *cites.org*
Hubbs-SeaWorld Reasearch Institute. *hswri.org*
IUCN/The World Conservation Union. *iucn.org*
Marine Mammal Protection Act of 1972. *nmfs.noaa.gov/pr/laws/mmpa/*
Marine Mammal Stranding Network. *nmfs.noaa.gov/pr/health/networks.htm*
NOAA Fisheries Service. *nmfs.noaa.gov*
SeaWorld Busch Gardens **Animals** Web site. *SWBG-Animals.org*
SeaWorld & Busch Gardens Conservation Fund. *SWBG-ConservationFund.org*
The Society for Marine Mammalogy. *marinemammalogy.org*

*Available at SeaWorld. Call **(800) 25-SHAMU** and press 46 to request an Educational Resources Catalog.

Index

A
Amphipods, 88, 48, 51, 61, 109

B
Baleen, 4, 21, **22**, 22, 23, 49, 50, 54, 55, 84, 90, 109
Baleen whales, 3, 4, 5, 6, 8, 9, 10, 11, 14, 15, 16, 17, **18**, 19, **20**, 20, 21, **22**, 22, 23, 24, 25, 28, 29, 30, 31, 32, 35, 39, 41, 41, 42, 43, 44, **48**, **49**, 50, 58, 60, 63, 79–87, **90**, 90, 91, 94, 95, 98
Barnacle, **24**, 25, 60, 64, **87**, 87, 109
Beluga whale, see *Whales*
Birth, 22, 23, 25, 47, 57, 66, 79–81
Blowhole, 5, **18**, 18, 19, **20**, 20, 29, 30, 42, 59, 62, 87, 109
Blubber, 15, 34, 35, 47, 49, 55, 79, 81, 90, 93, 109
Blue whale, see *Whales*
Body shape, 16, 35
Bottlenose dolphin, see *Dolphins*

C
Calf, 2, 5, 22, **41**, 41, 45, 57, 61, 66, 79, 80, 82, 99, 109
Callosities, 18, **24**, 25, 109
Convention on International Trade in Endangered Species of Wild Fauna and Flora (CITES), 75, 98
Coloration,
  countershading, **26**, 27, 68, 70, 109
  disruptive coloration, **26**, 27, 70, 110
Communication, 28, 41, 43, 44, 57, 103
Conservation, 91, 92, **96**, 96–98, **100**, 100, 101, 102
Counter-current heat exchange, 35

D
Diet, see *Food and feeding*
Disease, 86, 96
Diving, 30, 32, 33, 54, 56, **57**, 59, **63**, 63–65, 69, 89, 102
Dolphins, 3, 5, 7, 15, 19, 23, 29, 31, 38, 39, 85, 90, 91, 94, 98, 99, 101, 104
  Amazon river dolphin, 7, 8, 21, 23, 29, 47, **97**, 97, 108
  baiji, **7**, 8, 19, 29, **72**, 72–73, **93**, 93, **95**, **97**, 97, 102, 109
  boto, see *Amazon river dolphin*
  bottlenose dolphin, **2**, 8, **12–13**, 20, **28–29**, 30, 31, 38, 46, 47, 50, **68**, 68–69, **69**, **78**, 78, **81**, 84, 86, **87**, 94, 98, **102**, 106, 107
  Commerson's dolphin, 5, 9, 14, **15**, 16, 27, 79, **80**, 80, 81, 106
  common dolphin, 29, **40**, 40, 92, 94, 98, **103**, 107
  dusky dolphin, 39, 40, 106
  Franciscana, 7, 19, 108
  Ganges river dolphin, 8, 19, 29, **95**, 97, 108
  Hector's dolphin, 5, 14, 97, 106
  Indus river dolphin, 8, 19, 29, **95**, 97, 108
  Irrawaddy dolphin, 19, 107
  northern right whale dolphin, 98, **99**, 107
  Pacific white-sided dolphin, 39, 47, 98, 107
  Risso's dolphin, 25, 98, 107
  rough-toothed dolphin, 101, 107
  spinner dolphin, 39, 91, 98, 107
  spotted dolphin, **27**, 81, 91, 98, 106, 107
  striped dolphin, 39, 92, 94, 107
  susus, see *Ganges and Indus river dolphins*
  tucuxi, 8, 107
Dorsal fin, 3, 16, 17, **18**, **34**, 35, 56, **58**, 60, 62, 64, 67, **70**, **72**, 72, 74, 85, **103**, 110

E
Echolocation, 28, 43, **45**, 45–46, **46**, 67, 89, 110
Endangered species, 57, 58, 59, 71, 72, 73, 74, **75**, 91, **93**, 93, 94, **95**, 95, 96, 97, 98, 102
Endangered Species Act (ESA), 57, 59, 71, 75, 95–96, 97
Eyes, 21, 28, 29, 72

F
Fin whale, see *Whales*,
Flippers, 3, 16, **18**, 20, 25, 27, 30, **34**, 35, 38, 58, 59, 62, 68, **72**, 72, 85, 110
Flukes, 16, **18**, 30, **34**, 35, 38, **39**, 54, 56, **57**, 58, 62, **63**, 85, 86, 110
Food and feeding, 5, 10, 20, 22, 23, 30, 33, 41, 48–51, **51**, 55, 56, 57, 58, 59, 60, 61, 64, **67**, 67, 69, 73, 85, **86**, 86, 93, 94, 96, 104

G
Gestation, 57, **79**, 79, 110
Gray whale, see *Whales*

H
Habitat, 8–9, 64, **68**, 68, 73, 91, 93, 94, 101, 102, 110
Hair, 2, 22, 25, 29
Hearing, 28, 46, 57
Hubbs-SeaWorld Research Institute, **42**, 43, 85, 102–103
Humpback whale, see *Whales*

I
International Whaling Commission (IWC), 57, 94–95

114

IUCN/The World Conservation Union, 61, 75, 96–98

K
Killer whale, see *Whales*
Krill, 48, **49**, 55, 56, 57, 110

M
Marine Mammal Protection Act (MMPA), 57, 95, 104
Marine parks, 44, 45, 47, 66, 70, 78, 84, **87**, 89, 98–100, **99**, 103, **104**, 104
Migration, **10**, 10–11, **11**, 54, 61, 79, 85
Mysticetes, see *Baleen whales*

N
Narwhal, see *Whales*
Nursing, 2, 49, 81–82, **82**

O
Odontocetes see, *Toothed whales*

P
Parasites, 25, 38, 60, , 86, 87, 88
Pollution, 73, 92, 93
Population, 15, 44, 48, 57, 58, 60, 61, 63, 66, 67,70, 71, 72, 73, 74, 75, 83, 84—85, 86, 90, 91, 93, 94, 95, 96, 101
Porpoises, 3, 3, 5, 7, 15, 19, 23, 38, 85, 108
  Dall's porpoise, 79, 90, 94
  finless porpoise, 17, 102, 108
  harbor porpoise, 47, 81, 83, 90, 97, 101, 108
  vaquita, 5, 8, 14, **74**, 74–75, 91, **92**, 95, 97, 108
Predators, 27, 47, 66, 69, 70, 85, 86, **86**, 93

R
Respiration, 2, 3, 19, **20**, 20, 30, 32, 47, 56, 67, 80, 86
Rorqual, 8, 16, 17, 19, 20, 21, 22, **31**, 50, **51**, 106, 111

S
SeaWorld & Busch Gardens Conservation Fund, 101–102, **102**
Sexual maturity, 78–79
Size, 5, **14**, 14–15, **15**, 31, 35, 38, 39, 54, 56, 58, 60, 62, 64, 66, 68, 70, **71**, 71, 72, 74
Sleep, **47**, 47
Social behavior, 5, 25, **38**, 38, 39, **40**, 40, 43, 44, 69, 71, 89, 111
Stranding, 51, 64, 65, 67, 75, **88**, 88–89, 98, 99, **100**, **102**, 102, 103, 110
Swimming, 16, **17**, 25, 30–31, 35, 41, 47, 49, 59, 67, 80, 81, 82, 85, 86, 87, 88, 91

T
Teeth, 3, 4, 5, **18**, 22, **23**, 23–24, 25, 41, 49, 62, 64, 73, 83, 84, 87
Thermoregulation, 34–35, 111
Throat grooves, 20–21,**21**, 50, 60, 87

Toothed whales, 3, **5**, 5, 7, 8, 9, 11, 15, **18** 18, 19,**20**, **23**, 23, 25, 28, 29, 30, 31, 32, 33, 35, 39, **40**, 40, **41**, 41, 42, 43, 44, **45**, 45, **46**, 46, 48, 49, 50, 60, 62, 66, 72, 78, 79, 80, 81, **82**, 82, 83, 86, **88**, 89, **90**, 90,**92**, 93, 94, 95, 98, 102

V
vaquita, see *Porpoises*
Vision, 28–29, 41
Vocalization, 41–43, **42**, **43**, 44, 45, 55, 58, 66, 103

W
Whale,
  Baird's beaked whale, 90, 107
  beaked whale, 7, 15, 16, 17, 19, 20, 21, 23, 33, 38, 41, 81, 89, 107–108
  beluga whale, 7, 16, 17, **19**, 19, 23, 47, **52–53**, **66**, 66–67, **67**, 79, 80, 81, 96, 89, 93, **96**, 97,108
  blue whale, 5, **14**, 14, 17, 22, 25, 27, 30, **31**, 38, 39, **56**, 56–57, **57**, 80, 81, 84, 85, **86**, 97, 106
  bowhead whale, 8, 22, 35, 46, 50, **54**, 54–55, **55**, 84, **95**, 97, 106
  Bryde's whale, 8, **11**, 11, 98, 106
  Cuvier's beaked whale, 33, **64**, 64–65, **65**, 90, 107
  dwarf sperm whale, 7, 98, 107
  false killer whale,8, 29, 85, 89, 90, 98, 106
  fin whale, **4**, 81, 84, **85**, 91, 97, 106
  gray whale, 1, 6, 8, **10**, 11, 16, 17, **18**,**18**, 20, **21**, **22**, 22, **24**, 25, 29, 30, 31, **39**, **41**, 47, 48, **50**, 50, **51**, 56, **60**, 60–61, **61**, 81, **83**, 84, **87**, 87, 89, 95, 96, 97, 98, 99, **100**, 106
  Hubb's beaked whale, 25, 107
  humpback whale, 16, 18, 25, **34**, 38, **39**, 44, 49, 51, **58**, 58–59, **59**, 87, 97, 106
  killer whale, 8, **9**, 16, 17, **18**, **23**, 25, **27**, 31, **34**, **36–37**, **39**, 40, **42**, **43**, 44, 45, **47**, 47, **48**, 48, 49, 51, **70**, 70–71, **71**,**76–77**, 78, 79, 81, **82**, 82, 85, **86**, 89, 90, 93, 96, 97, 98, 103, **105**, 107
  melon-headed whale, 90, 101, 107
  minke whale, 22, 49, 84, 85, 89, 91, 98, 106
  narwhal, 7, 11, 16, 19, 24, 86, 89, 108
  northern bottlenose whale, 33, 90, 108
  pilot whale, 16, **45**, 47, 81, 85, **88**, 89, 90, 107
  pygmy killer whale, 90, 85, 98, 107
  pygmy sperm whale, 7, 98, **99**, 107
  right whale, 5, 6, 8, 17, 18, 20, 21, 22, **24**, 25, 30, 49, **51**, 54, 80, 84, 90, 91, 97, 106
  sperm whale, 5, 7, 8, 11, 15, 16, 17, 18, 19, 20, 21, 23, 25, 30, **33**, 33, 38, 39, 40, 42, 45, 46, **62**, 62–63, **63**, 79, 80, 81, 83, 89, 91, 94, 97, 98, 107
Whaling, 14, 55, 57, 59, 61, 63, 67, 82, 84, 89–91, **90**, 94, 96

115

Goals of the SeaWorld Education Department

Based on a long-term commitment to education, SeaWorld strives to provide an enthusiastic, imaginative, and intellectually stimulating atmosphere to help students and guests develop a lifelong appreciation, understanding, and stewardship for our marine and aquatic resources. Specifically, our goals are...

- To instill in students and guests of all ages an appreciation for science and a respect for all living creatures and habitats.
- To conserve our valuable natural resources by increasing awareness of the interrelationships of humans and the environment.
- To increase students' and guests' basic competencies in science, math, and other disciplines.
- To be an educational resource to the world.

> "For in the end we will conserve only what we love.
> We will love only what we understand.
> We will understand only what we are taught."
> —B. Dioum

Want more information?

If you have a question about animals, visit the SeaWorld/Busch Gardens ANIMALS Web site at *SWBG-Animals.org*

The SeaWorld Education Department has information booklets, teacher's guides, posters, and DVDs available on a variety of animals and topics. Call (800) 25-SHAMU, then press 46 to request an Educational Resources brochure.

Anheuser-Busch Adventure Parks

SeaWorld Orlando
(800) 406-2244
7007 Sea World Drive
Orlando, FL 32821-8097

SeaWorld San Antonio
(210) 523-3608
10500 Sea World Drive
San Antonio, TX 78251-3002

SeaWorld San Diego
(800) 257-4268
500 Sea World Drive
San Diego, CA 92109-7904

Discovery Cove
(877) 434-7268
6000 Discovery Cove Way
Orlando, FL 32821-8097

Busch Gardens Tampa Bay
(813) 987-5555
3605 E. Bougainvillea Ave.
Tampa, FL 33612

Busch Gardens Williamsb
(800) 343-7946
One Busch Gardens Blvd.
Williamsburg, VA 23187-87